By What Authority?

By What Authority?

The Churches and Social Concern

Anthony Harvey

scm press

British Library Cataloguing in Publication data

A catalogue record for this book is available
from the British Library

0 334 02849 3

First published in 2001 by SCM Press
9–17 St Albans Place London N1 0NX

SCM Press is a division of
SCM-Canterbury Press Ltd

Typeset by Regent Typesetting, London
and printed in Great Britain by
Creative Print and Design, Wales

Contents

Preface

During the seventeen years in which I was a Canon of West-minster I found myself a member of a number of commissions and working parties concerned with issues of public policy. I often asked myself what exactly, as a Christian theologian, I was expected to contribute. In an ethical committee, for example, set up by the Royal Navy to monitor the testing (with human beings) of escape devices for submerged submarines, and staffed by experts in medicine, physics and law, what was I supposed to offer? There is a New Testament text which might seem apposite: 'He who would save his life shall lose it'. But quoting this would hardly have helped their work forward. Nor did they need me to lecture them on the virtues of prudence and compassion. So was it just that my training and my beliefs might help them to clarify their own thinking and values?

My first attempt to answer this question took the form of a course of lectures in the Jerusalem Chamber at Westminster Abbey. I am grateful to those who came to listen to me for their attention and their stimulating questions, and I hope they will find this book an adequate fulfilment of the promise I gave them to provide some record of what I said. I am also indebted to Sir Richard O'Brien, the Chairman of the Archbishop's Commission on Urban Priority Areas, for scrutinizing the pages on *Faith in the City*, and to Dr Bernard Hoose of Heythrop College for doing the same with regard to Roman Catholic social teaching. Above all I must thank Dr John Bowden, who generously encouraged me to complete the project and carefully read the whole typescript, making many valuable suggestions. I need hardly say that though they helped me to avoid many errors and

contributed some welcome improvements I remain entirely
responsible for the imperfections which inevitably remain.

A. E. Harvey
October 2000

I

By what authority?

The twentieth century was different from any other in the church's history in that it saw the publication, in increasing quantities, of official church comment on social and economic questions. It was not that Christians had been uninterested in these matters previously, or had failed to bring their faith to bear on them. Indeed in the seventeenth and eighteenth centuries some notable Christian thinkers had joined in what was essentially a philosophical debate on what was then called 'political economy'. Moreover the nineteenth century saw a movement in England that was to have important social and political consequences, namely Christian Socialism. But thinkers such as F. D. Maurice who led this movement addressed themselves primarily to their fellow Christians in the church: their reasoning was based on propositions that were held to be true as articles of the Christian faith but were not necessarily assented to by the general population. By contrast, Roman Catholic social teaching (which effectively began with Pope Leo XIII's encyclical of 1891, *Rerum Novarum*) based itself, not on specific revealed doctrines, but on the widely shared philosophical tradition of Natural Law, and so was able to command the attention of people outside the Roman Catholic Church. This set in motion a process of Vatican social and economic commentary which continues to this day and has the strength of a consistent and continuous line of thought. In due course a similar approach was adopted by other churches. As the ecumenical movement gathered strength in the first half of the century, questions of social and economic justice established themselves firmly on the agenda. The ecumenical Oxford conference on 'Church,

Community and State' (1937) made a major attempt to tackle
these issues theologically, and the same issues have remained a
high priority for ecumenical work ever since; and in the last
decades of the century individual denominations began to set up
committees and churn out reports as a matter of course on every
kind of social and economic question, from unemployment to
prisons, from urban deprivation to the ethics of investment and
banking. The century truly became one of laboriously compiled
statements and reports, each of which could have been given the
title, 'The Church and . . .'.

The problem

What is the justification for this flood of comment by religious
people on matters which clearly lie outside their specific competence as church members? What basis exists in the Christian
faith for making authoritative judgments on matters such as
genetic engineering or financial policy which clearly lie well
outside the scope of the historic religious tradition? The reports
and encyclicals seldom address this question directly. Church
of England reports (like those of other non-catholic churches)
normally include an obligatory theological chapter; but the
influence of this on the rest of the text is usually negligible,
despite the protestations of the committee members that they
have been guided by theology all along. There is regularly
some appeal to the Bible: but exactly how writings at least
two thousand years old can be expected to give guidance to
the solution of specifically twentieth- or twenty-first-century
problems is a question rarely tackled. Catholic statements, by
contrast, tend to use the Bible simply for illustration and for
apparent confirmation when an appropriate text can be found,
and base the argument on more philosophical principles derived
from Natural Law. But again the question arises how far a philosophical tradition which had its origin in the early Middle Ages
can shed light on peculiarly modern problems, given that it relies
principally on an understanding of the nature and dignity of the
human being created in the image of God, but has few resources

to take account of the immense changes in our understanding of ourselves which have taken place in the last two centuries. In short, neither a biblical nor a philosophical approach seems to have the necessary robustness for launching an authoritative critique of modern society; and some of the presuppositions underlying both have been rudely called into question by the work of liberation theologians from Latin America, even though these, again, have often resorted to a biblicism which is demonstrably naive in the light of modern critical study of the Bible.

Part of the problem is created by the question of the audience to which this social commentary is directed. In this respect the Roman Catholic Church has shown a clearsightedness denied to others: its official statements are addressed 'to the faithful', and can therefore assume agreement on the truth of Christian doctrine. The Church of England, by contrast, conscious of its responsibilities as an established church, tries to respond to demands to give 'leadership' in a range of moral issues and to address the results of its deliberations to a wider public. But this immediately raises the question of its authority to make any statement at all. If the purpose is to contribute to the public debate on, say, unemployment, it will not do to base arguments on propositions (such as 'He who seeks to gain his life will lose it') which are not generally accepted outside the churches. But in that case what has a church to offer which deserves the attention of others? For this is the dilemma: if specifically Christian insights are invoked, the wider public cannot be expected to accept the argument; if they are avoided, why should anyone pay attention to what these church people are saying? It is notable that even Roman Catholic documents, which have the advantage of appealing to a philosophical tradition which has adherents outside the churches, and which usually address an explicitly Christian constituency, nevertheless seldom introduce considerations of a distinctively Christian character. At most, there is an occasional shy reference to the probable necessity of 'sacrifice' by some to achieve a situation of greater social justice for all.

The question was ostensibly faced up to in the *Faith in the*

City Report (1985), of which the subtitle was *A Call for Action by Church and Nation*. The main body of the report was divided into two parts, one addressed to the church, the other to the nation. This should have allowed considerable freedom in constructing the argument: the nation could be addressed in simple moral terms such as most people would agree with – and in fact the main emphasis of the report was on the 'grave and fundamental injustice' being suffered by that part of the population which (largely unknown to the rest) was subject to the multiple deprivations that had grown up in 'Urban Priority Areas' (UPAs). The church (to which the greater part of the report was directed) could then be confronted with a challenge based on explicitly theological premises. But in fact the 'theology chapter' prefaces *both* the 'church' and the 'nation' sections; and in the 'church' section such theological material as is invoked to support the key propositions that the church should be *local*, *outward-looking* and *participating* is banal and easily compressed into half a page. The primary basis of the 'Call for Action' to the church, as to the nation, remains the appeal to rectify a situation of 'grave and fundamental injustice' which manifests itself in the maldistribution of the church's historic resources as much as in the social and economic inequalities so apparent in the UPAs.

This apparent failure of theological nerve was widely criticized at the time: why had not the Commission confronted the church with a powerful theological vision of the task which lay before it as it resolved to 'stay in' (rather than abandon) the deprived inner cities and urban deserts of England? Those who made this criticism might perhaps have reflected more deeply on the case made in the report for such a vision to arise out of, rather than to be imposed from outside upon, church communities in inner city areas. Accordingly the 'theological chapter' was more concerned to clear a space for such 'local theologies' within the academic discipline of theology and to encourage new explorations than to construct a template (based on concepts such as 'Kingdom of God') to which such theologies should conform. It was hoped in this way to encourage the growth of an authentically 'urban' theology – and to some degree this hope has been fulfilled in the years that followed.

The example of *Faith in the City* is instructive in another respect. The Commission contained members or consultants who personally endorsed a radical Christian critique of the capitalist structures which had (at least in part) caused much of the acute deprivation they had witnessed, and who believed that the report should give strong expression to a more explicitly 'Christian Socialist' vision (it should be remembered that the Commission was working in the early years of the Thatcher government and in the aftermath of serious riots in Liverpool, Birmingham and Brixton). This was opposed from within the Commission, not on theological or ideological grounds, but out of sheer pragmatism. The members had witnessed conditions of acute deprivation and suffering that were largely ignored by the majority of English citizens. Their very first priority was to make urgent recommendations to both church and state which, if implemented, might bring some light and hope into UPAs. Presenting a radically alternative vision of society, however theologically correct, would have ensured that the report would have no practical effect, at least in the short term. The urgency of the situation, and the amount of confidence placed in the Commission by those who had been visited, made it seem imperative to come up with recommendations that were politically and economically practicable in the immediate future. In the event, the report achieved some success in practical terms; but not without a sense felt by at least some of the commissioners that their Christian principles had been compromised by the pressure of humanitarian pragmatism.

These examples illustrate some of the hazards to which any exercise in 'political theology' is exposed, and which seem not always to be recognized by members of committees set up by churches to investigate and report on new social problems. But a still greater difficulty is that of establishing a sound theological and philosophical basis on which a practical church critique of contemporary social trends can rest. We shall see in later chapters how precarious this theological basis can be when we

look at some recent church statements; but for the present
we must look at the alleged sources of authority for Christian
comment – the Bible and the (mainly philosophical) tradition of
the Western church – to see how far they are capable of sustaining the arguments that are allegedly built upon them. We begin
with the Bible.

The Bible

To the outsider, it might seem odd to claim that the Bible, no
part of which was written less than nearly two thousand years
ago, is capable of giving authoritative guidance in the twenty-
first century on questions such as the control of multinational
corporations, the ethics of investment or the control of the
media. Yet this claim is routinely made in church reports on
these subjects, and is rendered more plausible by the use of
certain strategies. One of these is to say that although the world
is of course vastly different from that of the biblical writers,
some factors remain always the same and biblical texts relating
to these provide a sound basis for conclusions that will extend to
new fields of enquiry. One example of this might be thought
to be crime and punishment. The reality of the human proclivity
to prefer crime to law-abidingness was as apparent to the biblical writers as it is today, and therefore what the Bible says on the
subject can be expected to retain its relevance and authority.
And certainly there are abundant sayings in the Wisdom tradition condemning dishonest and criminal activity and there is an
elaborate code prescribing the penalties attached to various
offences. This code is regularly appealed to when (as in the Ten
Commandments) it lays down generally acceptable principles,
or when it contains provisions which some particular group
wishes to see enforced today (as with the laws on homosexual
intercourse in Leviticus). But on the crucial question of punishment it turns out to be totally unhelpful. Not only does it enjoin
the death penalty for a number of offences which have not been
thought to deserve severe punishment at all since the Middle
Ages, but it does not officially recognize what is today the

commonest form of sentence, namely imprisonment (there are no references to prison in the Old Testament and those in the New Testament reflect the influence of foreign – mainly Hellenistic and Roman – institutions). Nor does it throw any light whatever on the question which is of greatest concern to all prison reformers, which is how to reconcile the differing claims of retribution, deterrence and rehabilitation in any penal system.

A famous use of this strategy, though in this case it resulted in the rejection rather than the acceptance of a biblical injunction, was in the formation of the church's attitude towards investment. The Bible clearly disallows usury; and it could be said that this, like 'crime and punishment', is a constant in human affairs. Lending money for interest has been a perennial activity. If it is outlawed in Scripture, surely this should remain valid for believers at all times. But the discovery of the Americas in the sixteenth century, with the consequent flood of bullion into Europe, the growth of a mercantile class and the expansion of business interests to new countries and continents created a situation entirely different from that of the self-contained rural communities of the early biblical period where the prohibition of usury had been a support for social cooperation and stability. Even in the New Testament there are signs that it was being widely circumvented or disregarded; by the seventeenth century the churches had tacitly agreed that it was no longer applicable in modern conditions. The 'unchanging' activity of money-lending had turned out to have changed a great deal after all.

A more sophisticated strategy has been to recognize that the Bible cannot be directly applicable to issues that had not yet arisen when it was written, but to argue that it contains principles which can be applied to these issues even if they had not been envisaged when the principles were formulated. One can ask, in effect, 'What would the Bible have said?' even if one cannot point to anything strictly relevant which it does say. A particularly striking example is offered by the institution of slavery. Both the Old and the New Testament take slavery for granted and offer no encouragement to work for its abolition. As a result, those who wished to see it preserved had no difficulty in appealing to the Bible for evidence that the institution was divinely sanctioned. Their opponents, however, rejected the proposition that slavery was a perennial factor of human society, and inferred from other texts (notably Paul's arresting statement that in Christ there is 'neither slave nor free') that the will of God was for a society in which personal freedom was equally available to all and that slavery in its modern form must be abolished. But that their view ultimately prevailed should not be taken as an example of good exegesis overcoming bad. It remains true that the biblical writers took slavery for granted and offered no challenge to it. The driving force for change lay in social and philosophical movements in the seventeenth and eighteenth centuries; and, as so often in debates of this kind, both sides felt able to invoke Scripture for their support. The argument that the biblical writers *would have* said such and such is always precarious and too often dictated by the *parti pris* of those who advance it.

Yet if the difficulties of applying Scripture to the problems of the modern world are fairly obvious to most reflective Jews and Christians, it remains true that a large number of believers continues to attempt a literal application. The turn of the millennium saw substantial groups of Christians making provision for the imminent end of the world as a result of their literal interpretation of prophecies in the book of Revelation. The establishment of the State of Israel half a century earlier was similarly greeted by fundamentalists of both religions as a fulfilment of divine promises presaging a new era – and in neither case did the failure of events to conform to the expected denouement do much to shake believers from their faith in the literal applicability of the Bible. For lurking behind attitudes which may seem to more liberal and sophisticated members of these faiths to be merely naive stands a menacing question. If the words of Scripture are not held to be literally true, what becomes of their authority? If their application is subject to the judgment of interpreters who bring their own 'secular' presuppositions to them, who is ever to believe that they must be taken seriously? The Bible, for example, explicitly condemns homosexual practices. If this is disregarded on the grounds that 'circumstances are now different' or that 'our understanding of sexuality has changed', how can we ever be sure when biblical commands are to be obeyed? Those who take a 'liberal' view of such matters do not always realize that the onus is on them to show how, on their reading, the Bible preserves its authority and can still be appealed to as a guide for conduct and decision. If they fail to do so, they can legitimately be challenged to say in what sense they believe it to be the Word of God and divinely inspired. They may also be properly accused of basing their 'Christian' judgments, not on any distinctive religious foundation, but on their own common sense and possibly world-corrupted judgment.

Natural Law

This brings us to the other main source of conviction which has customarily led Christians to make pronouncements about public affairs – the philosophical tradition of the Western church, usually referred to as Natural Law. The basic presupposition of this system, which was adopted by the Western church ultimately from Aristotle and more immediately from the Stoic philosophers of the Roman Empire, is that the nature of human beings, when properly understood as created by God in his own image, allows us to infer the conduct which is fitting for such beings and enables us to construct a moral code such as characterized the Christian community from its very earliest days – indeed it is confidently asserted that this philosophical tradition, far from colliding with revelation at any point, is constantly confirmed by it: the moral injunctions laid by St Paul on his readers, for example, are totally consonant with the findings of Christian moral philosophy (indeed the biblical critic may say that in any case St Paul got them from a popular form of Stoic philosophy, rather than from any recollection of the more radical moral teaching of Jesus). On the basis of this tradition it is claimed that the Christian faith provides its adherents with a sound basis for making 'Christian' judgments on quite technical questions affecting society today.

The adequacy of this method received perhaps its most stringent test in the case of the encyclical *Humanae Vitae* (1968). The procedure was to build on what can be inferred from the *nature* of human beings in their sexual aspect. The sexual organs are clearly designed for reproduction; therefore, according to the traditional teleological account of natural phenomena, any use of them for another purpose is *unnatural* and therefore (according to traditional Natural Law reasoning) morally wrong. Meanwhile, however, the opportunities for non-reproductive intercourse have dramatically increased since theories of this kind were formulated, and the churches (including the Roman Catholic Church) have come to acknowledge the relational, as well as the reproductive, function of sex: through their intercourse the married couple grow closer to one another at a deep level, and sexual activity between them is seen as a gift of God for purposes other than the begetting of children. This shift in the understanding of the significance of the sexual act, which can be charted in the marriage liturgies of all the major churches, indicates a corresponding shift in the understanding of the human being in its sexual aspect which should fundamentally influence the philosophical and theological arguments that can be built upon it. But to general astonishment, and in the face of expert advice to the contrary, Pope Paul VI in 1968 issued an encyclical which reaffirmed the traditional Natural Law argument based on a reading of human nature that allowed for 'relational sex' to be enjoyed only during the (difficult to calculate with certainty) monthly infertility period of the wife.

This example raises the question, implicit in all Natural Law reasoning, of the status of any statement about 'human nature' which is used to support the reasoning which will lead to a judgment whether a certain act is right or wrong. Human beings who now have the capacity to diagnose the sex and health of a foetus, to modify the genetic composition of living beings, to so lengthen life expectancy that the world's population could become unsustainable, or (by contrast) to set off a series of nuclear explosions which would make the earth uninhabitable, clearly do not have exactly the same 'nature' as those for whom none of these things was possible. Inferences based upon it must therefore be liable to change as further developments occur; but who is to judge which of these alleged changes is sufficiently fundamental to affect moral reasoning? Where is the authority which can continue to invest this form of reasoning with cogency? These are questions, again, which are seldom addressed in church statements and reports; but a failure to do so is bound to raise the suspicion that the authors are invoking the tradition in order to give divine authority to conclusions which they have reached on other, perhaps pragmatic, grounds.

Liberation theology

A notable jolt to all such reasoning was delivered in the 1970s by liberation theology. The Latin American theologians were the first to allow serious space in theology for the discipline (so important to Karl Marx, hence the label 'Marxist' superficially placed on them by their opponents) of the sociology of knowledge. Theology had always been done almost exclusively by moderately secure and adequately provided-for monks, scholars and senior clergy. Suppose a new start were to be made by men and women who were either at the very bottom of the social pile themselves or else had deliberately identified themselves with the poor? Might different priorities emerge and different meanings be found in familiar texts? Might the hidden bias in traditional theological categories suddenly come to light? By challenging the received tradition, might not these theologians at least stimulate a reappraisal of some traditional positions?

The effect of this on traditional exegesis of the Bible could be startling. Take the familiar story of Jesus and the Rich Enquirer (Mark 10.23–27), in which Jesus startles his disciples by saying that it is easier for a camel to pass through the eye of a needle than to enter the Kingdom of Heaven. On the face of it, this is a radical judgment on any form of personal wealth, only mitigated by what Jesus seems to add by way of a possible exception: with God all things are possible. Almost unanimously, commentators on this passage have passed lightly over the radical condemnation and homed in on the 'exception', which is deemed not to be an occasional possibility but to indicate the free grace of God routinely bestowed on all who open themselves to it: 'Jesus points to the miracle of divine grace' (Eduard Schweizer) is a typical interpretation. It took a liberation theologian to expose this 'bourgeois exegesis' and invite the reader to take seriously the plain meaning of Jesus' words. If the audience were the really poor, how natural for Jesus to assure them that they were the appointed inheritors of the Kingdom, the rich having far too many material preoccupations to qualify – unless, by way of exception (and it would surely be really exceptional), God made what is humanly impossible into a possibility for some particular individual. So much for a biblically based 'gospel for the rich'!

But the target was not only biblical exegesis: traditional theological affirmations could be shown to be equally vulnerable. For example, there was an ancient line of theological thought, going back at least to St Augustine, on the permissibility of the use of force in the face of violent aggression and injustice. This had been applied exclusively to the problem of armed aggression carried out by 'princes' and military leaders: the necessity to re-establish order, to punish the offender and to restore a situation where injustice had been remedied, though it was subject to a number of conditions if the warlike enterprise was to be 'just', was believed to take priority over the otherwise non-violent and 'pacifist' implications of the gospel. But suppose now one were to argue (as these liberation theologians did from their own experience) that 'violence' might be inflicted on large numbers of people, not by force of arms, but by the sheer oppressiveness of the power of the rich over the poor? Suppose there were such a thing as 'structural violence', by which the privileged few were able to exploit the impoverished many and cause untold human suffering? Might this not be an equally legitimate occasion for Christians to respond with some degree of violence? Was not the mobilization of popular resistance, normally non-violent, but occasionally even supported by force, a proper extension of the Just War doctrine, even though such action had never before been envisaged as proper for Christians? In short, was not a key but hitherto shamefully neglected concept of theology none other than *liberation*?

Traditional theologians had little difficulty in countering this radicalism by arguing, with some justice, that the situation in most 'developed' countries was vastly different from that in Latin America, and that this theological approach had, at best, no more than local validity. But the effect of this episode has nevertheless been profound. It will never again be possible to assume that theological truth and theological reasoning is the possession of a single cultural milieu. Alongside a continuing Latin American school of liberation theology (which has had an observable influence on many Christian and even some Jewish thinkers) the idea of 'local theologies', which would have different methods and priorities from those of the classical Western tradition, has taken root in several parts of the world ('Water Buffalo Theology', Korean 'Minjung Theology' and others) and was encouraged even in the highly traditional context of English theology by *Faith in the City*.

By what authority?

Given the inherent weakness and problematic methodology of all these approaches, what authority can the church appeal to when it makes its pronouncements on matters of public policy and social and economic life? In practice, it relies heavily on an existing moral consensus: despite the increasingly pluralistic character of modern society there is a stubbornly continuing agreement that certain values must be retained and promoted. Politicians can assume support for the proposition that society should be 'compassionate' and 'caring'. Respect for the freedom of the individual, the availability of education and health care to all, the requirement in public life and business that promises should be kept and corruption outlawed – all these can be assumed to be values generally shared throughout society. Above all, there is an obligatory attitude of support for 'human rights', with a corresponding public vigilance (especially among young people) to detect any form of discrimination on the grounds of gender, race or class (endemic though such discrimination continues to be in many areas of social life). When theologians enter public debate on current moral issues, and when churches issue statements and reports, it is to this degree of consensus that appeal is principally made, religious people seeing themselves as a kind of watch-dog against the intrusion of false values, as allies of the conscience of right-minded people, and as 'experts' only in the sense that their own theological discipline has equipped them to handle general principles and abstract concepts at least as well as, and in some cases better than, the more specialized professionals alongside whom they are working.

Theologically, a contribution along these lines looks rather thin. But this needs to be set in the wider context of the history of political thought. With the end of the medieval consensus that rulers were ordained by God and their authority therefore not subject to human scrutiny, came the Renaissance interest (going back to Aristotle) in the various possible forms of government and the growth of a primarily philosophical discipline known as 'political economy'. The first great exponents of this (Grotius, Locke and others) were Christians; but by the nineteenth century alternative philosophies were available, and the subject was pursued by Marx and his contemporaries with a passion born of the confidence that their thinking could have a practical influence on the form of regime under which their contemporaries and successors would live. But the churches were slow to react to this tide of new political thought, and where they did so their reaction was mainly negative: they found themselves regularly on the side of the status quo and opposed to the revolutionary movements of the time. The emerging Christian Socialism of some English theologians did not take up the philosophical debate but started from theological postulates (creation, incarnation, Body of Christ) and proclaimed on the basis of faith rather than reason the possibility of an alternative structure of society. Meanwhile Roman Catholic social teaching, with its deep and instinctive loyalty to the tradition of

Natural Law and its profound mistrust of any form of socialism (mainly on the ground of its traditional doctrine of the inviolability of private property) was insulated from any effective dialogue with secular philosophers. 'Political economy', as an inspiration for social reform, gradually disappeared from the scene, to be replaced by a never-ending debate between two schools of political philosophy, on the one hand some form of socialism and on the other a fundamentally conservative attachment to the status quo, the high intellectual ground being slowly taken over by economists. The argument becoming either increasingly technical (economics having achieved the status of a professional discipline inaccessible to outsiders) or increasingly political (quite modest proposals for reform being immediately labelled as either 'collectivist' or 'right wing'), Christian thinkers found it difficult to re-enter the debate save on grounds that they were confident would be acceptable to a wider constituency – that is to say, the moral consensus on certain broad principles which was supported by people of good will whatever their religion or background.

Is the situation any different today? Many people might say that it is even more difficult, given (as they would argue) the virtual disappearance of a moral consensus sufficient to warrant a Christian (or any other religious) contribution to public debate. It is certainly true that there is less place for a specifically Christian or 'theological' contribution than church people are regularly led to believe by their leaders; but I believe that Christianity, along with other religions, can still play a significant part in the formulation of public morality and policy. The grounds for this assertion will be discussed later; but first we need to look at some recent church interventions on the social and economic scene. The weaknesses we shall see there may provide clues towards establishing a more robust approach for Christians and others to adopt.

2

Faith in the City and
The Common Good

The Archbishop's Commission

There is, we have said, nothing new about Christian theologians contributing to debates on social and economic affairs. Indeed the earliest post-Renaissance political philosophers were mainly Christians who explicitly appealed to their faith in support of their arguments. Moreover, since the beginning of the last century, official Roman Catholic teaching has regularly included comment on such matters, and Anglican and Protestant churches have not been far behind. Yet the publication of the report of the Archbishop of Canterbury's Commission on Urban Priority Areas, *Faith in the City*, in 1985 was something new: the report was *unanimously* approved by the General Synod of the Church of England, it sold an astonishing 24,000 copies, it aroused considerable political controversy and its publication was still being celebrated ten years later. No comparable church statement or report had ever attracted so much attention or been followed by so much action. What enabled it to create this quite exceptional impact?

To answer this question we need to recall the circumstances in which it was written. Conditions in England's inner cities and outer housing estates (comprised in what had become known as Urban Priority Areas, an inelegant term invented to cover both) had begun to cause concern in the later years of the Labour government of the 1970s, and had been analysed in a White Paper in 1977. Six indicators of acute deprivation were used to identify these areas, and the characteristic which they most notably shared was described as 'multiple deprivation'. The Conservative government elected in 1979 continued to give attention to the problem, which was brought starkly to the public's attention by riots in Brixton, Toxteth and Handsworth. Meanwhile the churches were undergoing something of a crisis in their urban organization. Many Nonconformist churches had already withdrawn from inner city areas; Church of England parishes were struggling to adapt to massive shifts in population (some finding themselves with a mainly Muslim or Sikh population), inappropriate Victorian buildings and extremely demanding working conditions for the clergy. Roman Catholic churches were suffering from similar difficulties. Under pressure from a group of Anglican urban bishops, and by way of fulfilling a pledge given in the House of Lords that the Church of England would 'stay in' the inner cities, Robert Runcie, then Archbishop of Canterbury, set up a commission to report within two years. The result was the publication in December 1985 of *Faith in the City: A Call for Action by Church and Nation*.

On what grounds did the Commission have the confidence to issue such a 'call'? It possessed, first, the undoubted experience and skills of its members, only a third of whom were clergy, the rest drawn from the fields of the social sciences, education, social work, housing and voluntary organizations. No previous enquiry into urban living conditions had mustered so much expertise. Second, the team was resourced by a distinguished and able lay chairman, an experienced civil servant as secretary (seconded from a government department) and by some expert consultants. Third, and perhaps most important, the visits paid by the commissioners to a range of heavily deprived areas inspired in them a degree of conviction, if not passion, which was apparent in the report and enhanced its effect in many quarters. Their principal finding, reinforced by their evident care in assessing the evidence and their competence in interpreting it, was that UPAs were victims of *a grave and fundamental injustice*. It was a message which, delivered with the authority possessed by the team and its members, could hardly fail to excite the interest and indeed the compassionate concern of a wide public.

But my concern in this book is to identify the *theological* grounds on which church judgments are made on social and economic issues. With similar resources, it is arguable that any commission, whether or not of 'the church', might have come up with an equally compelling judgment on the state of the inner cities. What was the distinctive element which this church group of 'experts' was able to bring to their analysis? The simplest answer to this question is simply that the report was addressed to 'the church' as well as to 'the nation'; it was therefore required to take account of the *raison d'être* of the church and its mission in order to make credible recommendations – that is to say, it had to show a grasp of theology alongside the other disciplines involved. But this was only part of its task. Nearly half the report was specifically concerned with public policy, and made a direct appeal to government for reforms that would (it was believed) improve the lot of those whose 'deprivation' had been so vividly witnessed. What was their authority for doing this?

The answer appears to be that their appeal for 'justice', and their carefully presented account of the state of injustice being experienced, unknown to the majority of the population, by the residents of UPAs, was self-authenticating. The Commission had been unusually well placed to observe and report on the 'multiple deprivation' that had been caused by social and economic trends in recent years, and no further argument was needed to impress on the public the urgency of the situation. Indeed, even in its Appeal to the church, the Commission knew this to be by far its strongest card.

> There is a sense [it wrote] in which no further 'theology' is required. The Commission has had the opportunity of observing a concentration of human suffering at our doorstep of which the great majority of Church members (like the majority of our fellow-citizens) appears to be unaware. It should be sufficient to sound the alert: there is a clear demand on us all to come to the aid of those who have fallen so far behind the relative prosperity enjoyed by the rest of us. (§3.4)

So far so good. The problem arises at the next stage. Had the

Commission contented itself with diagnosing the problem and offering an expert analysis, no further justification would have been needed. But it went further, and proposed changes in public policy which, it believed, would ameliorate the situation. What authority did it have to do so? Again, the most plausible answer follows from the professional qualifications of the commissioners and the unusual opportunities they had had to observe and analyse the evidence. It could hardly be said that they were not 'experts': they were exactly the kind of people whom government ministers would normally draw into consultation when planning legislation. They were, that is to say, in as good a position as anyone to forecast the effects on UPAs of any practicable government action, and if the remedies they proposed did not always prove to be the best, that did not make them any different from other trusted government advisers. In any case the grounds of their recommendations were simply an application of the general principle of rectifying an injustice. On the possibility of reducing mortgage tax relief, for example (a proposal which was in fact adopted by the Labour government soon after it was elected), it wrote,

> It is unjust to tell those in bad housing that we cannot afford to do anything for them, that there is no money available to provide them with a home, and at the same time to give subsidies to those on the highest income. (§10.98)

It is true that these proposals were put forward without being 'costed'; but this was hardly the Commission's business. It was for government to consider them and investigate their practicability within its total social budget, if necessary giving them priority over other departmental expenditure. The essential thing was that they should be grounded in accurate observation and sensible consideration of consequences – and this the team was well qualified to do. Indeed the virulent criticism which the report aroused among politicians was seldom directed against the accuracy of its analysis. 'That *wicked* report', as Mrs Thatcher was overheard to describe it in private conversation, could not be rubbished as uninformed or unintelligent. The criticism of it as 'Marxist' (by politicians) or 'collectivist' (by an archdeacon in a letter to *The Times*) showed that the implications of this quite moderate appeal to social justice were seen as a threat to the freedom and property of relatively well-off individuals and evoked a predictable political reaction.

The same appeal to 'justice' (this time in its more technical judicial sense) was made in the chapter on 'Order and Law'. It is worth quoting the relevant sentences in full.

> The whole Bible reminds us that, left to themselves, neither the legislature nor the judiciary can be relied upon to create and maintain conditions in which justice will always prevail, and an objective standard is required against which to measure their procedures. Christians relate their standards of justice to their understanding of the justice of God; *but these standards are for the most part ones which are shared by the majority of their fellow citizens.* The distinctive service of the Church is to challenge, in the name of God and his justice, all human institutions and procedures when they appear to be falling short of these standards. [§14.5.1, my italics]

Once again appeal is made to a general moral consensus: standards of justice are 'shared by the majority of one's fellow citizens'. But where do these standards come from? There are strong grounds, philosophical as well as theological, for believing that justice is something other than what is actually held to be legal according to the laws of a state, and provides a standard against which any existing law or penal procedure may be measured. For many centuries of Western history it was taken for granted that this 'justice' derives from God and is to be interpreted by the church. In modern times a secular alternative has been vigorously sought, though without any general agreement as to its basis. When Christians claim to be able to base their understanding of justice on their knowledge of God they are making a perfectly legitimate move in the argument, and cannot be refuted by the success of any alternative explanation. Nor does this lead them into conflict with 'secular' understandings of justice. It simply provides them with a coherent framework of belief from which to exercise the role of vigilance which may be expected of them.

In one respect, however, this chapter of the report goes further. In the face of the contemporary tendency towards 'a more punitive approach to sentencing', and the removal in 1983 of 'rehabilitation' from the objectives of imprisonment stated in the Prison Rules of 1964, the commissioners felt bound to emphasize the faith of Christians in 'the infinite worth of every individual in the sight of God and the infinite possibilities of God's forgiving love' (§14.5.2). The balance that must be achieved between the retributive, the deterrent and the rehabilitative purposes of judicial punishment is a notoriously difficult problem, and a statement of Christian doctrine cannot be expected necessarily to influence penal policy makers. But again, there is a wider consensus to appeal to. The same section of the report continues,

> prison staff, probation officers and social workers would probably find it impossible to continue their work in a humane way if they abandoned all expectation of some kind of response in at least some of their fellow citizens who are convicted of crime.

Here, at least, the 'theology' is explicit, but its appearance is justified by an appeal to the natural instincts of those most closely involved. As so often, Christian conviction coincides with a wider moral consensus. Its explicit formulation is a legitimate strategy for bringing the weight of Christian opinion to bear on a discussion which must necessarily take place today in a 'secular' environment. The fact that in the decade following the report's publication penal policy was dictated by the political judgment that 'prison works', and that the prison population rose by an astonishing *50 per cent* (without any apparent effect on the rate of crime), so that Britain now has a larger proportion of its citizens incarcerated than any other European country save Portugal, only goes to show how necessary this Christian contribution may be.

If the criticism aroused by the section addressed 'to the nation' was that the policies proposed were unduly 'socialist' (not to say Marxist!), the Christian constituency was more critical of the 'theology' – or rather the alleged lack of it. It is true that part of the 'theological chapter' appeared to be somewhat defensive, in that much space is devoted to making the case for the Christian religion having the right and the duty to speak on matters such as these. In the face of a widespread view, held particularly by politicians of the Right, that religion is a totally separate matter from public affairs and that theologians should confine themselves to 'spiritual' matters, it seemed necessary to demonstrate that this view depends on an analysis of the human being as having a 'soul' separate from the 'body' which is now philosophically as well as theologically discredited. In any case there are some biblical and theological concepts which are certainly relevant in a social context. The fact, for example, that the future hope is expressed in terms not of a rural picture of Elysian Fields (as in classical paganism) but of a city – the new Jerusalem – is a natural one to allude to when evaluating city life today. The Kingdom is another concept which recurs again and again in social and political theology; similarly 'the Body of Christ' is an essential theological description of the church. All these make their appearance in the course of the report. But what the critics were objecting to was the apparent absence of a fully worked-out 'theology of the city'. No attempt is made to draw out from biblical and theological resources a schema of what, under God, a 'city' is intended to be; the most that is offered is the observation that the particular density and animation of city life provides an exceptional opportunity for the cultivation of those civic and social values which are close to the very nerve of Christian living. Apart from this, and apart from the fundamental 'call' issued to both church and nation to rectify a flagrant injustice, the one point at which theology is brought to bear is in response to the growing recognition among social workers, law enforcement officers and others of the need for 'community'. Given the vagueness of this concept and the multitude of definitions which can be found in the specialist literature it seemed appropriate for the church to offer its own understanding of that particular form of 'community' which is at the heart of the Christian experience. This is a point to which we must return later on.

But the theological chapter itself contains a robust defence against the charge that the theology was 'thin' or 'weak'. After arguing at some length for the relevance of theology to social and economic affairs it proceeded to give a solid reason for *not* attempting a comprehensive 'theology of the city'. This was that any such theology ought to come out of, rather than be imposed upon, congregations in UPAs. The significant influence here was liberation theology. This had demonstrated that a theology appropriate to particular social and economic conditions could be formulated by local people in a way that was authentic to their situation. Until then, academic theology had been the province almost exclusively of people in more comfortable circumstances; now, the 'poor' themselves had found a theological voice and demonstrated the possibility of formulating the Christian faith in a way that addressed their immediate priorities. Surely the same could be true of the deprived urban communities in this country; and the greater part of the chapter is taken up with attempting to clear a space within the academic discipline to accommodate the theological insights that might come from this quarter. Had an 'urban theology' been worked out by the Commission, some would have found it acceptable, others not, and discussion would have been diverted from the real problems of the UPAs to a debate between theologians. Instead, the report aspired to encourage urban Christians to work out their own theology. Indeed their belief that this was possible was one aspect of that 'faith in the city' which the Commission had come to possess, and has been vindicated, at least in part, by the gradual appearance of 'urban theologies' in the following years.

It could be argued, therefore, that the apparent reluctance of this report to proclaim a 'theology of the city' was in fact one of its strengths. The appeal to the nation was on the grounds of natural justice; and that to the church was basically the same: the church's historic resources were distributed in ways which

favoured the ancient mainly rural dioceses which had considerably less need of them than the more recent urban ones, and this
was an evident 'injustice' which demanded redress – and has in
fact received it to some extent through the substantial sums
of money raised by the Church Urban Fund, one of the most
tangible and effective consequences of the report's publication.
That Christians should have a distinctive vision of what urban
life in modern times might become was by no means denied; but
it was insisted that this vision must grow out of the experience of
those whose discipleship was being tested amidst conditions of
considerable deprivation, and whose Christian witness was
often a source of inspiration to others, rather than being
imposed upon them by academic theologians. Indeed the real
intellectual weakness of the report was not so much theological
as philosophical. Given the evidently unjust situation which had
been analysed, the recommendations inevitably involved some
redistribution of property and revision of priorities in government expenditure. The Conservative government of the time
could not but see these proposals as 'political', by which of
course they meant 'socialist'; and in fact the Commission would
have done well to present them in the context of a more clearly
thought out political philosophy in which this degree of redistribution of goods and curtailment of individual freedom would
have been seen to be compensated by equivalent public benefit.
But this leads us to consider another major church contribution
to political debate which was published eleven years later by the
Roman Catholic bishops of England and Wales, *The Common
Good*.

The Catholic bishops

In October 1996 a general election was little more than six
months away, and there was a discernible feeling in the country
that political change was both desirable and inevitable. Much as
the Thatcher years had contributed to the revival of British
economic life, the social consequences of those policies were
causing increasing concern. The Roman Catholic bishops

decided that they would do right to issue a statement to the faithful, setting out the issues at stake from the point of view of Roman Catholic social teaching. In fact they were addressing others also. Their ideas were 'based on firm Christian principles', but were 'just as likely to appeal to people with no belief' (Introduction, p. 2). But they insisted that they were not telling people how to vote: 'We are not involved in party politics' (§2). And the justification for this claim, despite the number of political issues touched upon in the course of the document, was that all they were doing was applying to the present situation in Britain a tradition of Roman Catholic social teaching which was at least a hundred years old and the content of which would be a valuable resource to Christians when making up their own minds what policies to support and how to cast their votes. This tradition was heavily reliant on Natural Law; hence the claim that it would be of interest to those outside the church, since the appeal is to principles such as that 'society ought to be organized in such a way as to improve the lot of all its members' – something that 'most people feel' (Introduction p. 2). The document could not therefore be criticized as an opportunist exercise in social comment inspired by the imminence of an election: the teaching had always been there, and indeed could be referred to in order to elucidate what the bishops were saying. What was new was the project of applying it to the very particular situation of Britain at the end of 1996.

The document is entitled *The Common Good*, a concept which Bishop David Konstant in his Introduction claimed would be familiar to many British people though they 'may not have had a name for it before'. As a title, this was highly significant, though, as we shall see, the promise it contained was fulfilled only to a limited degree. The style of the document is a refreshing change from the magisterial tone of papal encyclicals, which make no reference to the existence of thinkers outside the Roman Catholic constituency. Indeed the bishops say they 'want to be open' in their approach and to 'listen to the ideas of other churches', to which they give grateful acknowledgment at the outset (§5) even though they do not subsequently refer to them.

Nevertheless they succeed in avoiding a tone of high dogmatism: it is recognized that the issues are complex and often admit of no simple answers. Indeed it would have been contrary to the tradition of Roman Catholic social teaching to offer precise recommendations in the style of *Faith in the City*. 'The Church's teaching authority', they write, 'is comprehensive in its scope, but limited in its immediate application. It is for individuals and groups to decide how best to apply it in particular circumstances' (§27). Nevertheless there are moments in the document when the bishops come remarkably close to making explicit criticisms of current political positions. The proposition, for example, that 'the further enrichment of the already wealthy must . . . eventually also improve the lot of the less well-off and the poor', so dear to the 'New Right', is rejected simply on the grounds of 'common sense' (§74). Similarly, it is stated (§95) that 'Employers are not entitled to negate the right to join a trade union' – on the grounds, presumably, that this is an inalienable right, though this is not argued, and shortly before it was said only that 'trade union activity is *sometimes* a necessary corrective to managerial policies' (my italics). In general, however, the Roman Catholic tradition is observed of avoiding specific political issues; for 'some elements' in the teaching are 'direct applications of the moral law and therefore strictly binding on consciences. Examples would be the Church's condemnation of genocide or the deliberate encouragement of racial hatred' (§27) – a claim that sounds oddly to a generation more conscious than ever before of the church's dismal record over many centuries of anti-Semitism and the persecution of native peoples such as the Amerindians.

On what basis, then, do the bishops make their case for the promotion of 'the common good'? The term was defined by the Second Vatican Council (*Gaudium et Spes*, §26) as follows: 'the sum of those social conditions which allow individuals and groups to achieve their proper purposes more fully and quickly'. Note that this definition does not give social values priority over personal ones (as Aristotle did and as has remained a respectable view in political philosophy); indeed the same document affirms that 'the management of things should be subordinate to personal values and not vice versa', supporting this with Jesus' saying that 'the sabbath was made for man and not man for the sabbath'. It follows, therefore, that the 'common good' is satisfied when the rights of individuals are respected – and from this, as we shall see in a later chapter, flow considerable weaknesses in the argument for the existence of comparable obligations and responsibilities. But what are these 'rights'? Roman Catholic teaching is absolutely opposed to any form of positivism: these rights are 'in no way dependent for their existence on recognition by the state by way of public legislation'. Rather, 'they all flow from the one fundamental right: the right to life' (§37). Since this 'fundamental right' is presumably one which would be universally recognized (leaving aside for the moment awkward questions about the legitimacy of capital punishment or potentially lethal military operations), the bishops can claim to be arguing on the basis of Natural Law and to be making their appeal to the general conscience. It is true that in other places this claim is qualified by the statement that the rights flow from our understanding of man 'made in the image of God', and the view that his nature is essentially social is grounded in the highly theological proposition that God himself is 'social' (being a Trinity) and calls his human creatures to share in that social life (*Gaudium et Spes* §24; *Common Good* §18). Nevertheless, the fundamental appeal is one that can be made to anyone, even though the argument is also presented as one that requires Scripture for its ultimate authority.

But does Scripture give this authority? The Old Testament certainly does not envisage a situation in which everyone has a 'right to life': the Hebrews' criminal code had a number of crimes attracting the death penalty, and the treatment that they inflicted on conquered peoples (and which in some cases is represented as actually enjoined by God) involved the slaughter of men, women and children to an extent that is a world away from the modern concept of 'human rights'. So far as the New Testament goes, it would be difficult to marshal texts or instances in defence of the alleged 'right'; indeed Jesus' parables seem to be set in a society where this 'right' is routinely flouted (the murder of the servants of the owner of the vineyard, the vengeance of the king on the guests who refused his invitation) and it is taken for granted that a master has absolute rights over the life of his slave. Again, when we come to Natural Law, the notion of any absolute 'right to life' is limited by the occasional necessity of manslaughter in self-defence and the requirements of any criminal code which entails the death penalty (indeed the Roman Catholic Church has still not found it possible totally to discountenance capital punishment). The only principle which appears to be secure in church teaching is the absolute right to life of the *innocent* – and even this is subject to qualifications: if an operation is required for, say, cancer on a pregnant woman, it may be carried out even if there is a risk to the ('innocent') foetus; and (by the principle of 'double effect') the *indirect* killing of ('innocent') non-combatants, so long as it is unintentional and proportionate to the good obtained, is regarded as permissible. Thus even the duty to protect the innocent is not an absolute one; and even if it were it would certainly not be equivalent to that 'right to life' which is the foundation of the reasoning in *The Common Good*.

It appears, therefore, that for all their insistence on the rootedness of its principles in Scripture and Natural Law, the Roman Catholic bishops in this instance have relied more on the general moral consensus which finds expression in current formulations of human rights. We shall be looking at these more closely in a later chapter. But meanwhile it is worth noticing that other points in the document derive more from common sense and a generally shared morality than they do from specifically Christian belief. Observations such as that free market attitudes may conflict with public morality (§80) or that 'workers contemplating a strike have a duty to take account of the likely effect of their actions on other groups' (§96) do not require religious or philosophical justification: they could be made by any right-minded person. Moreover in the matter of ecology appeal is made to what is assumed to be a fundamental human instinct. 'Those who feel moved to a loving care for the internal balance of nature are responding to a deep religious instinct . . . their intuition tells them' etc. (§106). In this relatively new area of ethical thought no attempt is made to introduce Christian theology.

This is not to say that the bishops' document lacks wisdom or cogency. Indeed the analysis of the state of Britain in 1996 is perceptive and urgent, an authentic application to this country of the papal strictures on the dangers of uncontrolled capitalism and the free market economy. Yet it has to be said that, compared with *Faith in the City*, its challenge is muted. There is none of the passionate appeal for social justice which gave the Church of England's report such power and influence. There is the same recognition in both that the real curse of poverty in this country today is exclusion from the rest of society: 'The real "poor" in a relatively prosperous Western society are those without sufficient means to take part in the life of the community' (*Common Good*, §74). But whereas for *Faith in the City* this amounts to a scandalous injustice too little noticed by 'comfortable Britain', in *The Common Good* it is simply alluded to as something incompatible with Roman Catholic social teaching. The difference is admittedly one of style and presentation rather than content; but given that in reality both documents, as we have seen, rely more on the perceived moral consensus of the population than on specifically Christian doctrine, the explicit appeal of *Faith in the City* to a public sense of justice and compassion for the deprived may be said to reveal a wiser strategy. Both documents, however, fall far short of demonstrating the possibility of a distinctively Christian critique of social and economic affairs. We must now examine one or two more specialized church reports to see whether they can do better.

3

'The Theology of Work'

In a century of church comment on social and economic affairs it is not surprising that *work* should have had a prominent place. As John Paul II observed (*Laborem Exercens*, §3) the question of human work is 'a *constant factor* both of social life and of the Church's teaching'. Ever since the Industrial Revolution created the social phenomenon of large-scale unemployment, the provision of work by government or by charitable bodies has been seen as a high priority for Christian concern. The suffering caused by unemployment – not just through poverty but through loss of personal dignity and exclusion from a full life in society – has been seen as a social evil against which there has been insistent Christian protest. The protesters will of course have recognized that in some cases the unemployed themselves are responsible for their condition and that efforts must be made to persuade them to work; but it has been obvious to all but the most biased observers that the majority of the unemployed find themselves in this situation through no fault of their own, and only action by government, social agencies or wealthy well-wishers can materially help them. Unemployment, that is to say, is one, if not the principal, aspect of that 'grave and funda-mental injustice' which was brought to the public's attention by *Faith in the City* in 1985; but it had been recognized as a major social evil for many years before. The churches needed no new justification for raising their voices in protest against this demeaning condition in which a small but substantial propor-tion of the population has found itself in virtually every indus-trial and indeed post-industrial society.

Papal teaching

But if unemployment is bad, it seems to follow that 'work' is good; and it is this apparently self-evident proposition which has set theologians on a quest to find a basis in Christian doctrine for a positive evaluation of it. A systematic attempt to do this was made by John Paul II in his encyclical *Laborem Exercens* (1981). That ninety years had passed since *Rerum Novarum* without any such attempt being made may be explained by the preoccupation of earlier popes with the question of 'labour': the tendency of capitalist enterprises to exploit their workers seemed in their time to be the main social evil to be contested, and the value of work itself (as opposed to that of the worker) did not seem central to the issue. It is of considerable interest, therefore, to see how it is tackled in the first papal document which explicitly elaborates a 'theology of work'.

The first thing which needs to be said is that the encyclical, like virtually all authoritative Christian statements on the subject, treats the proposition that work is both good and necessary as self-evidently true.

The Church is convinced [we read that work is a fundamental dimension of man's existence on earth. She is confirmed in this conviction by considering the whole heritage of the many sciences devoted to man: anthropology, palaeontology, history, sociology, psychology and so on. [§4]

As a general statement this does not bear examination. History provides the example of classical civilization, doubtless along with other less well-known ones, where work was regarded as an affliction from which one should if possible be spared, and which should be left to a slave or servant class so that civilized people could devote themselves to more agreeable and humane occupations. For the Greeks and Romans, work was *ascholia negotium*, the 'denial of leisure', and so to be avoided by any cultivated person. History, that is to say, does *not* confirm the papal proposition; and doubtless anthropology is at least as

ambivalent. But this is not merely a matter of correcting an error
in the encyclical; the point goes to the heart of the matter. Is it
right to assume that work is always good, any more than (like
some of the ancients) to assume that it is always bad? 'Work'
includes labour and drudgery, words that carry negative moral
connotations; and if we add 'hard labour', then it is clear that the
spectrum must include activity which is very far from 'good'.

The pope goes on: 'But the source of the Church's conviction
is above all the revealed word of God, and therefore what is a
conviction of the intellect is also *a conviction of faith*.' It seems
to follow that if one's intellect is *not* convinced one can nevertheless have the assurance that Scripture establishes the point.
Unfortunately the point is not so easy to establish. The key text,
in *Laborem Exercens* and many other papal documents, is
Genesis 1.28: 'Be fruitful and multiply, and fill the earth and
subdue it'. It is admitted that these words 'do not refer directly
and explicitly to work', but it is stated to be 'beyond any doubt'
that they do so indirectly and implicitly (§4). It is said to be
'through work' that man 'confirms his dominion' over the earth
(which is taken to mean every part of the universe which is accessible to us). Indeed this activity is said to belong to the very
nature of man as created by God: 'Man is the image of God
partly through the mandate received from his Creator to subdue,
to dominate, the earth'. Admittedly these words were written
before today's ecological sensitivities had rendered them politically incorrect: there would now have to be a careful disclaimer
to avoid the imputation that the Bible could be invoked to justify
any raping of natural resources. Even so, the argument is somewhat precarious. 'Dominion' can be exercised by right of inheritance, by force of arms, or by reason of the sheer complaisance
of subjects. It *may* involve work, but again it may not. If it is
exercised by the philosopher king or the mathematician or the
potter it could be said that dominion over something is con-
ferred by work (though in the case of the last two the word
'dominion' is being stretched to breaking point) but in the case
of a South African mineworker or a child worker in an Asian
textile factory it would be more natural to say that work domi-

nates *them*. Yet this text is the entire basis for the claim that Scripture is the source of the conviction that work is a 'fundamental dimension of human existence'.

The point, however, is developed further. The account of Creation in Genesis 1 represents creation as a 'work' of God from which, on the seventh day, he 'rested'. If it is granted (though no proof is offered of this, and many theologians would strongly deny it) that man's 'work' is of the same nature as that of God, then it follows that, by working, human beings share in God's activity:

> Men and women who provide sustenance for themselves and their families in such a way that at the same time they employ their energies for the benefit of society are justified in thinking that by their own labour they advance the work of the Creator and benefit their fellow men, and that their personal industry contributes to the divine plan in history. (*Gaudium et Spes*, §34)

Hence the doctrine that human work is a sharing of God's creative work; but it is clear from this that not all work is so privileged. It must 'benefit our fellow human beings' as well as ourselves, and this proviso introduces considerable complications. An artist may give pleasure by his work, and so share God's creative work. But suppose he does not, and people turn away from his work in disgust: has he suddenly ceased to be a co-creator? A scientist's life-work of research may turn out to have deleterious consequences for others: is she likewise to be said not to have done 'real' work? It is already becoming clear at this stage of the argument that 'work' is a varied activity, and the same high theological value cannot be given to every form of it. Indeed the claim that human work is a sharing of the divine creativity may be plausible enough in the case of *creative* work, to which is added the proviso that it must be of benefit to others; but how much of most people's daily occupations can properly be so described? As Alan Richardson remarked (*The Biblical Doctrine of Work*, 2nd ed., 1963, p. 15), 'Talk about creative work is natural in bourgeois society . . . but it belongs to a different age to that of the Bible'.

At this point in the encyclical one is beginning to wonder why only this one text from Genesis is invoked to give scriptural support to a doctrine of work. For there is another which seems at least as relevant (and was in fact most frequently invoked by the Fathers): at their expulsion from the Garden of Eden Adam and Eve are told, 'Cursed is the ground because of you: in toil you shall eat of it all the days of your life' (3.17) – to which St Paul seems to be referring when he says that the earth 'was subjected to futility' (Romans 8.20). This text does in fact appear right at the end of *Laborem Exercens* (§27) and is given the following commentary:

> Sweat and toil . . . present the Christian and everyone who is called to follow Christ with the possibility of sharing lovingly in the work that Christ came to do. This work of salvation came about through suffering and death on a Cross. By enduring the toil of work in union with Christ crucified for us, man in a way collaborates with the Son of God for the redemption of humanity.

Notice that it is not said that Christ shared our 'toil and sweat' (for the only work he is known to have done is that of a carpenter: Mark 6.3, a statement modified in Matthew to 'son of a carpenter', 13.55). Rather, it is assumed that our toil and sweat are equivalent 'in a way' to 'suffering and death', so that it can be a means by which we share Christ's redemptive suffering. Once again, this is clearly stretching the meaning of 'work' far beyond its normal use: to speak of Christ's 'work of salvation' is not on the face of it to say anything about *toil*; and to claim that our 'toiling' is a form of collaboration with Christ in his 'work' is, to say the least, precarious (notice the defensive phrase, 'in a way'). Significantly, the English and Welsh bishops in *The Common Good* completely ignored this interpretation, but then went on to make the surprising statement, 'We would oppose an unduly negative view of work . . . as . . . a curse consequent upon the Fall' (§90). It seems they felt free to ignore a crucial biblical

text that happened not to be in accord with their view that 'work
. . . is a vocation, a participation in God's creative activity'!

It is true, of course, that there are more references to 'work' in
the Bible than this. A large number of professions is mentioned;
Jesus' parables presuppose a working community (how could
they do otherwise?); and St Paul, in the tradition of Old
Testament Wisdom literature, encourages industriousness and
rebukes idleness (2 Thess. 3.11–12). He also prides himself
on working to support himself financially in order not to be a
'burden' on his congregations (2 Thess. 3.8 and elsewhere). All
of these references (which dutifully appear in *Laborem
Exercens*, §26) show that work was understood as a necessary,
and in most cases honourable, occupation. But none of them
carries a positive value judgment on work itself; indeed in Jesus'
environment there were types of work which were distinctly dis-
honourable, such as tax collecting and (in some cases) shepherd-
ing. There are no New Testament texts from which it is possible
to infer that work is *good in itself*.

It seems, then, that the attempt to base a Christian understanding of work on the Bible is liable to lead to a dangerous
simplification, in that a great variety of human activities, by no
means all of them good, are subsumed into the single category of
'work', which is then defined as participation in the work of the
Creator. Fortunately Catholic teaching has for the most part
implicitly abandoned the attempt, and followed instead a more
ancient philosophical tradition which distinguished between one
kind of work and another, the most desirable being the purely
intellectual activity of the philosopher (*theoria*) and menial
work being fit only for servants or slaves. This distinction
between good work and menial drudgery has enabled it to make
a solid protest against the tendency of capitalist enterprises
(particularly in the nineteenth century) to treat 'labour' as a
marketable commodity and to insist on the 'rights' of workers
over against their powerful employers. But this insistence stems
less from a clear doctrine of 'work' than from a valuation of all
human beings as created in God's image (about which we shall
have more to say in a later chapter). It is in the light of the

inherent dignity of human beings that it is admitted that even
unemployment is better than some forms of work. As the
authors of *The Common Good* concede (§97), 'It is not morally
acceptable to seek to reduce unemployment by letting wages fall
below the level at which employees can sustain a decent
standard of living'. Grossly underpaid work, or work carried
out under inhumane conditions, is rightly condemned, whatever
the Bible may be alleged to say about 'work' being participation
in God's creation.

An ecumenical enquiry

The fact is that to make any useful contribution to the problems
of 'the world of work' in modern times it is important to
distinguish between different kinds of work – manual, artistic,
intellectual, pastoral and so forth. This the Roman Catholic
tradition seems to have signally failed to do, perhaps owing to
the constraint of having to relate its approach to some normative
text in Scripture. By way of comparison, it is instructive to look
at an ecumenical report published in the early months of 1997
(shortly before the general election of that year), *Unemployment
and the Future of Work*. The subtitle is *An Enquiry for the
Churches*, from which one might expect that the language would
be such as to address Christian people on the basis of their faith,
without an explicit concern for the extent to which it might
present a cogent argument to those outside the churches. In the
Preface, however, we read that it is 'offered to the Churches and
our nations [Britain and Ireland] as a prophetic word', and the
summary of its main findings (p. 174) includes highly political
recommendations such as more employment in the public sector
financed by higher taxation, and the establishment of 'a national
minimum wage'. The working party (just a quarter of whom
were clergy) was therefore confronted with the same dilemma
that we have seen in other cases: how were they to present a
distinctively Christian contribution in such a way as to be
regarded as serious participants in a public debate of national
importance?

One answer to this, and perhaps the most convincing one offered in the book, is given by David Sheppard, then Bishop of Liverpool and chairman of the ecumenical sponsoring group, who wrote in the Preface that 'a cry of pain' had been heard by the Working Party, 'a deep wound in the body, dividing those who are left out of decent opportunities from the favoured majority'. Such things, he goes on, 'call for costly, long-term measures. None of us could expect that such a deep wound could be healed without sacrifice'. Here the appeal is not to theology but to a generally held sense of justice. The language is that of *Faith in the City* (not surprisingly, since Bishop Sheppard was Vice-Chairman of that Commission), and the grounds of the appeal are once again a shared moral revulsion from a 'flagrant injustice'. He even goes so far as to demand 'sacrifice' from all in order to provide long-term remedies – which, as we shall see, is a distinctively Christian note that is remarkably rare in church documents of this kind and is not taken up at any point in the 'Enquiry' that follows.

The Working Party itself, however, was determined to offer a more sophisticated 'theology' than this. Indeed it concluded by saying,

> To be a member of this enquiry has involved a constant movement back and forth between our inheritance of faith and our experience of the plight of the unemployed and ill-treated . . . Time and again we have found ourselves driven back to the Bible, to our common experience in worship and to the teaching of our churches. (pp. 196–7)

So we look with interest to see what foundation for their thinking they have found in these sources. Right at the start of their report they quote some paragraphs written some thirteen years previously by Peter Baelz about

> the vision of the Kingdom [which] puts in question any social or economic system which allows the world to be divided into the powerful and the powerless, the rich and the poor, or

allows one group of people, whether a class, a nation or a group of nations to pursue its own welfare at the expense of the welfare of others. (Board for Social Responsibility, *Perspectives on Economics*, 1984, p. 76. pp. 2–3)

These may indeed be admirable sentiments; but their roots in Christian Scripture and tradition are by no means obvious. Where does the Bible speak of there being no 'divide' between powerful and powerless, rich and poor? There is of course much about the poor being protected, blessed and ultimately rewarded and the rich being *excluded* from the Kingdom. But the notion that the advent of the Kingdom will remove any such differentiation flies in the face both of the realism of Deuteronomy ('The poor will always be with you in your land', 15.11) and of the call of Jesus to poverty, which implies the existence of a genuine option to be rich. And where does the Bible (or, for that matter, Christian tradition until very recently) forbid a *nation* to pursue its welfare at the expense of others? The Old Testament prophets frequently look forward to a time when Israel will enjoy exactly such an opportunity to make up for the exploitation it has suffered at the hands of other nations; and the New Testament has nothing to say on such matters at all. And it would be equally hard to find an example in subsequent history of a 'Christian' nation subordinating its own interests to those of another. Peter Baelz's admirable vision seems, in fact, to owe more to a somewhat naive Christian political idealism than to any real foundation in the Christian tradition.

But the Working Party then goes on to put forward some theological findings of its own. With respect to 'work' it has three arguments (pp. 3–4):

1. The first is the standard reference to men and women being made 'in God's image', with the 'potential for creativity'. From this it is inferred (though the logic is not obvious) that 'the economy is there to serve human beings, not human beings to serve the economy' (a proposition that the Pope, as we saw, connected rather with the saying of Jesus about the sabbath being made for man, not man for the sabbath).

2. Jesus 'gave living expression to [love of others] as dutiful son fulfilling his family responsibilities to his mother, in services to family and community before his more public service as teacher and healer'. This, of course, is pure supposition: nothing is said in the Gospels about Jesus' activities before his public ministry. But from this dubious proposition inferences are drawn (again by means of a somewhat mysterious logic): the economy is 'one way in which society provides us with opportunities to serve one another and meet each other's needs'; and 'to work . . . is the way we are enabled to contribute to sustaining and transforming the world'. It is interesting that it is also admitted that work may be 'tedious, oppressive and exhausting'. It is not said, however, that such work may be disqualified from making its contribution to the noble project of 'sustaining and transforming the world'.

3. The third argument is based on a fundamental Christian doctrine: 'We do not have to do anything to earn the love of God; it is a free gift'. From this the surprising conclusion is drawn that 'no-one should therefore be excluded from paid work'. The logic here is so mysterious that it can hardly count as a serious theological argument.

Later in the same section there is one more appeal to the Bible:

4. 'It may be the conventional wisdom in the world of economic affairs that economic growth is the precondition of helping the poor and those at disadvantage. The Bible proposes a radical alternative . . . namely that only a just and caring society can achieve real and lasting prosperity' (p. 5). Here it is certainly the case that the Old Testament insists on justice and care for the poor and weak as a condition for God's blessing (which may well result in something we might recognize as 'prosperity'). The weakness lies rather in the claim that it proclaims a *radical alternative*. It has to be asked, why alternative? Why not accept that economic growth is necessary but then go on to ensure that there is justice and compassion as well? Otherwise, if the Bible's scheme is really an *alternative* to economic growth, why should we attend to

it as in any way authoritative over against the 'conventional wisdom' which in this case appears to most economists to be incontrovertible?

This last point raises a wider question, which seems to be recognized in the words which introduce this section of the Enquiry (p. 3): 'in describing and interpreting what we have learnt and in proposing a new way forward *we draw on particular narratives and images of scripture*' (my italics). This is developed in the final chapter:

> the resources our faith offer us . . . stories . . . of a human society reflecting the shape God gave to the world; a society where money and wealth and land are there for sharing, and where for that reason the firstfruits of the harvest, the first portion of all wealth, is to be set aside, a sign that all wealth comes from God.

This utopian picture suggests that there is more than one way of using the Bible. The texts we have discussed seem to rest on the assumption that it carries particular authority for Christians and has a rightful place in any argument that is intended to set norms for the churches to follow. But it can also be invoked (and this may be particularly appropriate when a wider audience is being addressed) by way of illustration and example. All will agree that the social and economic arrangements set out, say, in Deuteronomy 15 (remission of debt to the poor creditor, generous provision of loans and so forth) would, if carried through, produce a society very different from, and perhaps morally superior to, ours. To this extent there may be great value in drawing attention to it: it shows that ours is by no means the only possible economic system, and the vision it offers of freely accepted mutual responsibility and cooperation may be a genuine source of inspiration for social and political thought. The Bible, in other words, can provide a useful point of comparison, an alternative vision. But may there not be other classic writings that do the same? In the sixth century BCE the Athenian sage, writer and politician Solon introduced measures for the remission of debt and the narrowing of a dangerously wide gap between rich and poor and set out his policies in poems which might be equally inspiring for political thinkers to follow. Similarly, Karl Marx's *Das Kapital* has offered a powerful alternative vision to countless people during the last century. If the Bible is appealed to merely as an example, it has to compete with a number of other 'alternatives'. But, if not, something has to be done to demonstrate its continuing relevance to problems of which its writers can have had no inkling. The reasoning by which this is done needs to be more robust than any that we have looked at so far.

Not that the authors of this Enquiry sat light to theological method. On the contrary, they included a substantial essay on the subject as an annex to their main report (pp. 293–8). This rather dense piece of writing takes *Faith in the City* to task for falling between the two stools of a liberal 'Middle Axioms' approach and a genuine commitment to radical change such as would be promoted by liberation theology. We saw in the previous chapter that this problem was in fact recognized by the Archbishop's Commission, and that there were strong practical reasons for opting for a pragmatic approach. But it would be difficult to argue that *Unemployment and the Future of Work* comes out any better on this score. Its theological grounding, as we have seen, adds little to its basic appeal to a consensual concern for fairness and justice, and its recommendations (such as that for a statutory minimum wage) spring from pragmatic choices between frankly political options. Certain controversial assumptions, such as that *paid* work is desirable for all, and that the economic growth required for this is sustainable indefinitely, are accepted on the basis of technical arguments that have nothing to do with theology; and the focusing of these assumptions on the 'cry of pain' heard from the unemployed prevents the Enquiry from making any serious exploration, theological or otherwise, into the possibility of a radical redefinition of 'work' in a post-industrial society.

Varieties of work

For, if there is a weakness in church teaching such as in these
two documents, it is in their failure to undertake any such
exploration. The attempt to found a Christian understanding of
'work' on the Bible and Christian tradition is faulted from the
start when no account is taken of the very different connotations
of the word in the Bible (and indeed throughout history until
quite modern times) from those which it has in the world of
today. In Antiquity, and for centuries up to the Industrial
Revolution, 'work' was a relatively simple concept. For most
people it was manual (as for soldiers and slaves) or agricultural,
for some it involved skilled use of the hands in various crafts, for
a few it was artistic, and for a small and privileged class it was
what we would now call administrative, political or intellectual.
When it was hard (as it usually was), the agricultural worker
would see the force of the statement in Genesis that the land was
under a 'curse', exacting sweat and toil in return for its produce;
and economic conditions were such that all but the most privileged would be aware of the necessity of work for human
survival. Nevertheless there were forms of work which could
be seen to have greater dignity. If the 'work' of God when he
created human beings could be likened to that of the potter,
there was presumably a sense in which at least the work of artists
and craftsmen could properly be described as 'creative', a word
in popular use today to mark out those activities which seem
best to fulfil the human potential. But it is difficult to imagine
that Christian theological language about work 'enabling
human beings to be co-creators with God' would have had much
resonance with the vast majority of workers in Antiquity who
struggled to sustain themselves by unremitting manual labour.

A change came with the advent of technological means by
which the amount of physical effort required to produce arte-
facts (or indeed, in due course, to till the fields) could be drastically reduced. There seemed to be a promise that the curse on
the earth pronounced to Adam might now be lifted, or at least
mitigated, so that the human race would be able to obtain the
rewards of its work with far less exertion. In fact, of course, the

new technology was immediately used, not to reduce hours of work, but to increase the quantity, and in due course the variety, of products, to the gain less of the manual worker than of the owner, manager or entrepreneur. Work, for the majority, continued to be unremitting toil, only gradually made more humane by government regulation and the provision of social services of various kinds; for a small minority the same evolution produced considerable wealth, for the first time divorced from the inheritance or acquisition of land. It was to counter the inevitable exploitation of 'labour' in these circumstances that the churches first attempted to put forward a case for the 'rights' of workers, and in their thinking very properly concentrated on the *person* of the labourer, asking only that the *conditions* of work should be humane and in keeping with the dignity of the human being. How far the work itself conformed to a 'theological understanding' of what work is intended by God to be was seldom asked.

In more recent times the aspect of work which has preoccupied religious thinkers has been the lack of it. In an industrial society, where not just survival but success is linked to participation in economic activity that is based on 'labour', unemployment is rightly seen as a social evil that cannot be cured merely by the provision of adequate means of subsistence for the workless. It carries with it a measure of social exclusion that greatly exacerbates the poverty of the unemployed relative to the standard of living of their working neighbours. That a substantial number of people should be subjected to this demeaning condition in an otherwise affluent society is effectively represented as an injustice which any civilized country should seek to abolish, and church voices have repeatedly been raised to this effect.

We are now said (in the 'developed' countries of the world) to be living in a 'post-industrial' society, by which is meant the fact that the labour force (in the sense of unskilled workers) has greatly decreased and those who gain their living by non-manual and intellectual skills have become more than a small minority of the population. But this has by no means eliminated the scourge of unemployment. Politicians may take credit for having

reduced the total from, say, 10 per cent to 4 per cent; but that
smaller percentage still represents many thousands of fellow
citizens whose conditions of life should be a source of shame to
the rest – so long as (but only so long as) their lack of paid
employment continues to cause, not just relative poverty, but a
lack of self-respect, the virtual elimination of all possibility of
purposeful and fulfilling activity and even social stigma leading
to exclusion from much of civic life.

It is obvious (and the point has been taken up by a number of
individual theologians as well as by many social commentators)
that these consequences are not inevitable. It is a result of social
attitudes rather than of any iron necessity that deprivation of
paid work should cause such suffering. The point tends to be
ignored in Roman Catholic teaching, but is recognized in
Unemployment and the Future of Work where it receives exten-
sive discussion (pp. 72–81). There, however, a deliberate judgment is made that *paid* work is always preferable, and to answer
the question whether the provision of paid work for everyone is
a practical proposition and would be ecologically sustainable in
the long term, recourse is had to a (not necessarily impartial)
report by the International Labour Office in 1996 (*World
Employment*, 1996/7) and the conclusion drawn is, 'We have
heard nothing to convince us that decent paid work for all is
an impossible dream' (p. 79). As a result, the Enquiry pays
no further attention to the possibility of a change of public attitudes, an opening up of the 'voluntary sector' to 'unemployed' of
all ages or to the fairer distribution of paid work by the reduction of overtime and the extension of work-sharing. Though it is
recognized that there are great varieties of 'work', there is no
recognition of the fact that 10 per cent of all work in the UK is
voluntary; on the contrary, the objective of all public policy
should apparently be 'paid work', of whatever kind, for all.

The influence of theology

This somewhat simplistic approach, which is characteristic of
both Roman Catholic and other churches' thinking on the

subject, may perhaps be traced back to the malign influence of the alleged 'theology of work', in which the temptation seems to be to take it as given (in Scripture and tradition) that 'work' is *good*. This leads to a curiously naive analysis. In other matters we are accustomed to making distinctions. Money-making may be good or bad according to the way it is done and the purposes for which money is wanted; physical exercise, though normally good, may be harmful in certain conditions or when overdone; artistic creation can be perverted to yield only sensationalism. Few things are totally good or bad *in themselves*. Yet when it comes to 'work' theologians seem to assume that there is a value here which is good without qualification, except that it must 'benefit society' or even (in the most recent example) that it must be paid. This has led to an undue concentration on a very small range of biblical texts, and even to the dismissal of the clear implication in Genesis 3 that work is a consequence of the 'curse' pronounced on Adam after the Fall. By contrast, a more rounded use of Scripture might yield the following analysis of different kinds and attributes of 'work':

1. It is taken for granted in the Bible that work is necessary for survival (Gen. 3.17–19) and cannot be expected to be pleasant (Eccles. 2.22–23: 'What reward does anyone have for his labour, his planning and his toil here under the sun? His life-long activity is pain and vexation to him . . .') – though the author also says that one should make the best of it (Eccles. 3.22).

2. Idleness is condemned, for the good reason that it is anti-social: others will have to support the idler (Prov. 6.6–11 and *passim*; 2 Thess. 3.10) – which is also the reason why thieving is unacceptable (Eph. 4.28).

3. Work must be complemented by rest, as God rested after his 'work' of creation (Ex. 20.11) and ordained the sabbath rest which was fundamental to the Jewish culture. This rest, however, was not merely a space for idleness: it was a 'holy' time, marked by worship, celebration and festival, as in all ancient agricultural communities.

4. Beyond what is required for survival, work may be good or bad. Jesus ben Sirach (Ecclesiasticus), for instance is at one with the pagan philosophical tradition when he writes, 'The wisdom of the scribe depends on the opportunity of leisure; only the one who has little business can become wise' (38.24 – the whole passage is important for any account of what the Bible has to say about work, but is seldom referred to in official church documents, and was conveniently removed from consideration by Reformation theologians by virtue of being only in the Apocrypha). Moreover, most work that is done beyond the needs of survival is motivated by financial gain, and this motivation is *pleonexia* (covetousness), which St Paul regards as equivalent to idolatry (Col. 3.5). Alternatively, work may (and should) be an expression of *diakonia* (service), and is clearly good when it contributes to 'the common good' (Eph. 4.12 etc.).

5. Work deserves its reward, and it is a grave sin to withold wages unreasonably (Deut. 24.14–15; James 5.4; etc.).

But, in any case, may not all our troubles proceed from ever having thought there was such a thing as a 'theology of work'? Suppose we were to begin on more neutral ground and speak, not of work, but of 'activity'. It is clear that human activity may be good or bad according to its nature and its consequences; and if we concentrate on asking ourselves what it is good for human beings to be employed in, what best fulfils their nature and what contributes most to their own happiness and that of others, we may find that some 'work' is indeed participation with God's creation, but that other activities not normally classified as work (such as prayer) are equally so, and that much that goes by the name of 'work' is unworthy, dehumanizing and superfluous. Or again, we might usefully adopt an older philosophical category and speak, not of the value of work, but of the virtue of industriousness (about which there is much in the Bible as well as in the tradition of moral theology) to which we might usefully apply the Aristotelian concept of the 'mean', a virtuous industriousness being half way between idleness and overwork. We might attend to what is said about 'rest' in the Bible – the sab-bath rest of the Old Testament, the 'rest' promised for the people of God in the letter to the Hebrews – and reflect on Augustine's suggestion (*En. in Ps.* 92) that for God work and rest coalesce into one and that this is the state for which we are destined ourselves; and this provides an interesting comparison with the Elysiums, paradises and utopias of other traditions. We might bring the doctrine of original sin to bear on the question whether human beings are naturally lazy and require the pressure of poverty and the inculcation of virtue to overcome their sloth (as the Burkean tradition has held) or whether they naturally delight in work and come to hate it only because of arbitrary institu-tions and the unjust exercise of power (as has been the creed of utopian socialism). All this would be perfectly valid 'theology' with which Christian people may be helped to see how their faith relates to the realities of life today. But what, I suggest, we should not do is take from the world of contemporary dis-course a word such as 'work' (or 'crime' or 'sexuality' or 'family' or 'economics') – words which are already loaded with presup-positions derived from particular circumstances and attitudes (such as that work is good or that the creation of wealth is desirable) – and then dredge up material from the pool of Christian tradition (especially the Bible) to create a 'theology' of it, on the basis of which churches then presume to instruct politi-cians on how the affairs of the world should be organized. We would do better to base our argument on the simple appeal for justice with which Bishop Sheppard prefaced *Unemployment and the Future of Work*. But to approach the question along these lines we need a secure understanding of the nature of the human being, to which we shall return later. Meanwhile we must look at further areas in which the churches have sought to make a contribution to public policy and public debate.

4

Marriage, sex and the family

On the face of it, 'the family' is a topic that should present fewer problems than any of those we have looked at so far. Whereas questions such as the reduction of mortgage tax relief, or the right to strike, clearly lie outside the immediate purview of the Bible and Christian tradition, the relationship between the sexes and the ethics of family life might be thought to be a constant in social history. In these matters does human nature ever change? Is there any reason why what seemed right to the biblical writers should not seem right to us? Is not 'the family' (as Archbishop Donald Coggan used to say) at the very heart of the Christian – as indeed of the Jewish and the Muslim – religion? Why should there be any difficulty in applying the resources of our faith to questions of family life and intimacy today?

Yet in fact we find that it is precisely over these questions that individual believers and churches disagree with one another most profoundly. There is widespread rebellion among otherwise faithful Roman Catholics against the papal rulings over contraception and the exclusion of divorced people from the sacraments; disagreement over homosexuality caused a near-fatal crisis at the Lambeth Conference of 1998; and proposed changes in the Church of England's practice over the remarriage of couples when one of the parties is divorced threaten to open a long period of anxious discussion. If the sources of our faith were clear on these matters there would presumably be little scope for disagreement. As it is, the difficulties of inferring Christian practice from the norms of the past seem daunting; yet attempts are still made in officially sanctioned documents to offer a 'theology' of marriage and family life. Is there any justification for the enterprise?

Certainly, when considered carefully, the project presents formidable difficulties. Where, for instance, does one find the 'family' named in the Bible? The word hardly appears; what we find instead is the 'household', a larger social unit even than the extended family, comprising not just family relations over several generations but servants and slaves as well. This, and not the nuclear family of today, was the basic unit of society in Antiquity; and not only its size but also its organization set it a world apart from anything we now have in the Western world. Its structure was patriarchal, all authority rested with the senior male, and the transfer and acquisition of property were the governing factors in almost all marriages. Nor is it the case that the changed situation today can be regarded by Christians as simply the result of secular trends and as something which might be put into reverse. The equality of the sexes, the rights of children and equal opportunities for each member of the family are things which Christians have struggled for over the last century and which it would be against the conscience of most of them to reverse. The picture of family life presented in the Bible is not just antiquated: in many respects it is now judged to be actually wrong.

But even granted all this, can we not distil from the Bible certain more general principles about family life which can be claimed to have permanent validity? For example: Jesus was against divorce. On this there can be no question; his recorded sayings leave us in no doubt about the seriousness of his disapproval. How individual Christians and the churches they belong to are to witness to this clear moral principle is a matter for the churches to decide themselves; and the history of their attempts to do so shows how difficult a problem it is. Reconciling the demands of setting a clear example of life-long fidelity on the one hand and, on the other, showing compassion and pastoral care towards those whose marriage has failed demands some degree of compromise, and, not surprisingly, different churches have placed themselves on different points of the scale which stretches between rigorous discipline and pastoral flexibility. But in so far as the general principle – that divorce is undesirable – is one that may be said to be universally applicable, Christians have a perfect right to proclaim it on the basis of their religious convictions. When they do, they find themselves in company with the great majority of the population which also believes that divorce should so far as possible be avoided and supports government initiatives to discourage it, principally on the grounds of the damage it does to children. It is hard to see what distinctive contribution Christians can make to the public debate on the matter other than the strength of their conviction (which may result in practical action) that marriage is a lifelong commitment and that everything possible should be done to help people to maintain it as such. This, as we shall see, may in fact be their most valuable contribution; but it is a good deal more ordinary, not to say banal, than the promise of a 'theology of marriage' may have led them to expect.

Homosexuality

Much the same goes for another issue which is a subject of intense debate at the present time: homosexuality. We have an explicit condemnation of all homosexual acts both in Leviticus and in Paul's letter to the Romans, and those (and there are not a few in the churches) who instinctively repudiate homosexuality can appeal to these texts on the assumption that here is another area in which 'human nature is always the same'. But other Christians (now the majority in most churches in developed countries) find two flaws in this argument. First, the relevant texts are conditioned by the cultural presuppositions of their time and may not be literally applicable to the twenty-first century. Secondly – and much more important – this is an instance where, even if human nature is the same, our understanding of it is dramatically different. It is now established to most people's satisfaction that a homosexual orientation is, in many cases at least, the result not of an act of will but of genetic or psychological factors quite beyond the individual's control.

Consequently the Bible's stigmatization of it as a 'sin', implying that it is the result of moral choice, can no longer be accepted. Moreover the New Testament enjoins on us a principle that must surely override any inference drawn from the ancient codes of Hebrew law: any form of discrimination on the grounds of a condition for which a person has no responsibility – race, gender, class and so presumably sexual orientation – is flagrantly contrary to the ethic preached and acted on by Jesus, who deliberately sought out and befriended those whom society shunned.

As we saw earlier, disagreement among Christians over this issue is dangerously entrenched, and reflects an underlying unease about the status of Scripture as an authority for moral decision. If the clear statements on homosexual acts in both Old and New Testaments are disregarded, does this not open up a path of relativity and permissiveness which would deprive Christians of their right to make any judgments whatever on moral questions? This is a genuine source of anxiety which must not be minimized. At the same time, there are ways of using Scripture which offer a better handle on modern issues but still retain respect for it as a source of moral guidance. Consider, for instance, the way in which St Paul (or possibly a follower) offers a 'theology of marriage' in Ephesians 5. He is writing in the context of a culture in which the predominance of the husband and the subordination of the wife and children were taken for granted in any household. He does not directly challenge this – how could he, without appearing to distance himself from most people's idea of what constituted a decent and respectable family? Indeed he goes on to say, as his contemporaries would have expected, that a wife should 'fear' her husband (the literal meaning of the word which is tactfully translated 'honour' in most modern versions of Eph. 5.33). But at the same time he brings a distinctive Christian insight to bear on the marriage relationship: it should be marked by a quality of love which is both inspired by and an actual expression of Christ's love for his 'body', the church – a vision of marital devotion which has found its way in one form or another into almost every marriage liturgy performed by the churches. He states this (as he was

bound to do within the conventions of his time) as a project for
the husband; but the principle is such that in our changed conditions we may, indeed must, apply it equally to the wife: both the
partners should have the same vision before them of self-
sacrificial and mutual love. For Paul himself wrote in another
place that in Christ there is 'neither male nor female' (Gal. 3.28).
It is for us to draw out the principles underlying the teaching of
the New Testament and so lay bare its enduring message, shorn
of the limitations imposed by the culture of its time.

The use of Scripture

This is in fact how most instructed Christians probably use their
Bibles when confronted by moral problems; and in the case
of marriage, since a large proportion of weddings are still
performed in church, the results of this method are still attended
to at least once in their lives by a sizeable section of the population. Paul's theological insight into 'loving as Christ loved his
body, the church', and the biblical concept of 'covenant' as a
relationship which is more than contractual and binds the
parties together even when they fall into unfaithfulness towards
each other, undergird every Christian presentation of the nature
of the marriage bond and arguably contribute to the success and
happiness of many marriages. Can we not use the same method
with regard to the relationship between the sexes in general – in
particular extra-marital sex and homosexuality – in such a way
as to take account of modern circumstances and yet maintain
due respect for the authority of Scripture?

The difficulty here is to find any relevant texts that are not
totally conditioned by their time and circumstances. As we have
seen, explicit references to homosexuality occur, but are of questionable validity in view of our changed understanding of the
nature of sexual orientation. What of sexual relations outside
(or before) marriage? We can begin with at any rate one principle which seems to have enduring force. Adultery is always
wrong. In Old Testament times it was a criminal offence and
incurred the death penalty for both parties; in the time of Jesus

this had been mitigated by the legal condition that the act of adultery must have been 'witnessed' by two independent witnesses – an unlikely event which is the basis of Jesus' intervention to save a woman from the 'justice' of some over-zealous promoters of the letter of the law (John 8.2–11). But the offence itself remained a serious one, and would normally justify immediate divorce if the offender was a woman (the wife had less power to exact recompense from an adulterous husband). Modern society no longer regards it as a crime; but moral disapproval of it remains extremely strong – and this for good reason: it is an act committed by one of the marriage partners for his or her own gratification which will almost certainly have damaging consequences for the spouse and for their children. No religious authority is required to support its condemnation: adultery is contrary to the good of both society and individuals.

So much is taken for granted in the Bible. Indeed Jesus uses this assumption as a means to express his disapproval of divorce: it is *as bad as adultery*. It is when we try to look beyond this and find principles restricting sexual intimacy that we get into difficulties. In Jesus' time the opportunities for extra-marital intercourse were (by our standards) extremely limited. For a man to go with a married woman was adultery, which, as we have seen, was a criminal offence. To go with an unmarried woman carried great risks. If she became pregnant she would lose her chances of marriage, and her lover could be punished. The only safe course for the man was to go with a foreign woman (which may be the situation of the lover in the Song of Solomon: his beloved was 'black but comely') or a prostitute; and prostitution, then as now, was morally unacceptable – there are plenty of texts to this effect. The situation as it is today in the West, where sexual relations between unmarried persons of either sex may be enjoyed with impunity and with minimum risk of inducing pregnancy (and with easily available abortion when they do) is one which is totally strange to the Bible and to Western society through most of its history. We search in vain for texts which will allow us to make a 'Christian' judgment on it.

But if there are not actual texts, surely there are general

principles derived from the Christian faith which we can apply? Christian disapproval of extra-marital intercourse has, until recently, been universal, and 'keeping oneself pure' for one's eventual spouse, or else adopting complete celibacy, are still thought by most to be the Christian ideal, even if they are no longer the norm for most Christians. But on what is this based? It is agreed that prostitution is wrong–this is a general consensus, not a distinctive Christian insight. From this can be inferred an equally strong rejection of the commercial exploitation of sex – which again is a widely shared moral position. But given that the phenomenon we are concerned about – readily available extra- and pre-marital sex – was hardly a problem at all through most of biblical and Christian history, we should not be surprised to find that there is no clear guidance on it in either Scripture or tradition.

Today, Christian teaching on the subject usually takes the form of stating it as a fact that the purpose of our sexual faculties is fulfilled only within a loving, permanent and fully committed relationship, and that such a relationship exists only in marriage. A possible extension of this is to say that a homosexual relationship may be equally loving, committed and permanent and therefore an appropriate place for sexual intimacy; and many heterosexual Christians are now ready to make this concession to homosexuals. But where does this doctrine of total and lifelong commitment as a condition of sexual intercourse come from? Some would say that it is implied in Genesis: put together Genesis 1.27 ('Be fruitful and multiply'), Genesis 2.18 ('It is not good that the man should be alone') and Genesis 2.24 ('they become one flesh'), and you can argue that the power to bring new life into the world (the purpose of the sexual act) and the love of man and woman are two fundamental dimensions of human existence and cannot be separated. It follows that sexual intimacy is not intended to serve any other interest. As Basil Hume expressed it (in *The Tablet*, 27 August 1994, p. 1086), 'These two dimensions, the unitive and the procreative, cannot be artificially separated without distorting the true significance of the conjugal act itself.' But this argument rests on a cluster of assumptions. These texts nowhere speak of marriage, nor of exclusive relationships; indeed they were never understood in Jewish tradition to imply that divorce was impossible and that only one marriage partner was permissible (Jewish society was, after all, one that in early times permitted polygamy), and anyone wishing to argue that their meaning is confined to establishing the divinely ordained necessity of marriage for the continuance of the human race can hardly be refuted by reference to these texts alone. Nor does the Christian Natural Law tradition give us much help either, for the reason just given, that the question has only recently arisen in its modern form. In the face of an increasing tendency to talk about 'recreational sex', and indeed of the popularity of the phrase 'having sex' (which seems to imply that sex is an activity without any interpersonal implications whatever), it is an urgent matter for Christians and churches to set their insistence on life-long commitment on a firm basis. This, it seems, would have to be not so much theological as psychological and philosophical; but few theologians, let alone churches, seem to have accepted the challenge, preferring to leave the field clear for 'secular' thinkers.

The Church of England

In the light of all these difficulties, we look with interest to see what approach was adopted in one of the most recent church reports on the subject, *Something to Celebrate: Valuing Families in Church and Society* (Church of England, Board for Social Responsibility 1995). Once again, the title announces an ambitious project. The Church certainly needs frequent reminding of its responsibilities in the sphere of family life; but the report aims to address 'Society', which raises once again the question of the basis on which it has authority to do so. This question is never tackled; but even in its recommendations addressed to the church the Working Party (less than half of whom were clergy or theologians) recognized that there is no easy path from Scripture and tradition to the family in its modern form, for much the same reasons as I have set out already. The biblical texts require 'careful reflection' and 'wise interpretation' if they are to offer guidance (p. 75). The Genesis texts are quoted, and are said to embody the 'biblical ideal' of family life, but again without any recognition of the extent to which the required meaning is read into them; as for the many stories in the Bible which concern families, they offer an 'intense realism' which prevents us from being in any way sentimental about family life: if the family is 'crucial' in human history it is also 'marred by sin and human frailty' (pp. 76–7). The Ten Commandments receive more extended treatment: the 'sabbath rest' enjoined on the entire household is claimed as an important principle of family life, the prohibition of adultery and the command to respect father and mother are taken to be enduring principles encouraging marital fidelity and respect for the elderly (pp. 78–80). Turning to the New Testament, the authors claim that 'Jesus' opposition to divorce, for example [but what other "example" could they have found?], makes clear how highly he regarded the bond of marriage'; but this is immediately qualified by the recognition that 'many Christians accept that divorce and subsequent re-marriage may be the right way forward when a marriage has broken down irretrievably'. Apart from this, it is noted that Jesus upheld the Ten Commandments (he could hardly do otherwise and remain within the law of his country!) and had a quite exceptional regard for children and an unusually positive attitude towards women (pp. 80–2).

In the other writings of the New Testament evidence is found for 'the biblical insistence that becoming fully human and truly free is a social process' (p. 82). The cultural conditioning which renders so much of what the apostolic writers say on the subject inapplicable today is recognized: Christians are therefore liable either to regard it all as irrelevant or to try to 'get behind' Paul and the others to the 'original' teaching of Jesus. Both options must be rejected; instead the texts must be taken seriously at their face value, but interpreted with 'historical sensitivity and spiritual maturity'. An example of the process may perhaps be seen in what is said about Paul and family relationships: 'husbands were to love their wives, parents were to treat their children fairly, and masters were to rule over their slaves with justice'. So much is uncontroversial, and reflects a widespread moral consensus in Antiquity. But we then read (pp. 82–3) that 'Paul is concerned for reciprocity in household relations', which, if true, would represent a striking departure from the mores of his time. Unfortunately no instances of this are offered, nor could they be from the pages of the New Testament. 'Historical sensitivity and spiritual maturity' may not be reliable guides towards accuracy in reporting what is actually said in the Christian Scriptures.

The report then moves on to 'The Church's tradition'. Starting from 'the Christian understanding of God' and of 'mature personhood', the argument moves to the surprising statement that 'the Gospel impels us to accept the transformation not only of our inner life, but of the forms and patterns of our corporate life as well', yielding the conclusion (which is crucial to the entire report) that 'this cannot be taken to imply that there is only one form of the family which is right for everyone'. And if one wonders how this conclusion is reached from Christian sources, the answer appears to be that it is not: the 'wisdom' that is required is drawn from 'biology and what the natural sciences teach us . . . history . . . and what the humanities and social sciences have to say . . .' (p. 88). 'Theological perspectives' (the title of this chapter) turn out to be inadequate on their own to establish the case the authors are most concerned to present, namely that Christianity is not committed to any single form of family institution or intimate relationship. Indeed the very first of the recommendations which conclude the report states that 'The Church needs to recognize and value the different ways in which people live in families at the end of the twentieth century' (p. 210).

But is there then no criterion by which to judge whether any of these ways is in fact superior or inferior to others? It was the failure of the report to answer this question that predictably aroused strong criticism. Conservative Christians complained that there was 'no clear doctrine' of marriage and family life; liberals found little to add support to the positions they already held. The recommendations offered to both Church and Society were bland, and the really contentious issues (for the church as for society) were avoided. On the question of homosexual 'marriages', for example, which will soon need to be seriously addressed (it has been already in the USA), the report contents itself with 'welcoming continuing discussion of issues relating to gay and lesbian people' (p. 211, Recommendation 7); and its main conclusion relevant to public policy is one which needs little argument to support it, namely that poverty, poor housing and social deprivation are prime causes of marriage breakdown and that the increase of the divorce rate is a problem that cannot be tackled in isolation from these wider factors.

The Christian contribution

The claim, therefore, that 'the Christian tradition has great wisdom to offer' to those wrestling with ethical issues relating to the family seems barely vindicated by the conclusions offered in the report. In one sense, it is true, that tradition is perfectly clear: marriage is the only possible basis for family life, children should be brought up wherever possible by both natural parents, and divorce should continue to be regarded as inadmissible in a Christian community save (perhaps) on grounds of adultery. But Christians who live in the real world of today cannot easily accept these principles without qualification even for themselves, let alone as guidance for secular society. All will have friends and neighbours who are divorced and enjoying second marriages which are (by any reasonable standard) 'blessed'; all will know, or at least know of, single parent families where the upbringing of the children is at least as wholesome as in the homes of some married couples whose marriage is falling apart; all will have some experience, even if it is at second or third hand, of homosexual couples who are deeply committed to one another and whose claim on the church (if they are members) to receive some liturgical and pastoral acknowledgment of the 'covenant' they have entered into together must surely receive some recognition. All are asking for guidance from their churches on these difficult issues. How is the Christian 'tradition' to continue to speak authoritatively (even within the churches) in the face of these new circumstances? *Something to Celebrate* did little to reassure us that a theologically based answer is forthcoming or even possible.

That is not to say that it had no theological contribution to make. There were, for instance, two biblical points made which would have been capable of fruitful development. First, there was a reference to the Fifth Commandment, 'Honour your father and your mother'. This is a clear call for respect between the generations, and the report correctly sees its relevance to the breakdown of relationships between generations today. Unfortunately it fails to notice the social changes which make some reinterpretation essential: in Antiquity the expectation of life was much shorter, and the number of those who achieved 'grey hairs' was infinitely smaller than it is now; moreover in a relatively unchanging society, the 'elders' naturally enjoyed a reputation for wisdom by virtue of long experience, whereas today their knowledge and skills are rapidly overtaken by those of their children and even grandchildren. An entirely proper exhortation to the young to respect the old cannot so easily be based on this text.

The second point is the quite unusual, perhaps even unprecedented, regard which Jesus had for children. Giving priority to the interests of children over those of adults is in theory a common value of our society today. The UN Convention, and our own Children Act, all testify to the general public desire to see children given proper respect. But in practice things can be very different. For the first time, perhaps, in the history of civilization what might be called the 'covenant between the generations' has shown signs of breaking down. In the past it was taken for granted that parents would seek to give their children a better life and better opportunities than they had had themselves. They often underwent strenuous deprivation in order to save for their children's subsequent well-being, and much social reform was motivated by the passionate desire to see the next generation spared some of the hardships endured by the present one. But today we see the opposite tendency. By our own longevity we are bequeathing to our children a tax burden greater than any we have had to bear ourselves; to maintain our own standard of living we make them pay for their own higher education; we are leaving to them a host of unsolved and menacing environmental problems while securing our own ever-increasing standard of living; and we are seeing in many of our homes an unprecedented abuse of children and abandonment of them to their own devices in order to pursue our adult pleasures or even (in the deplorable case of 'home-alone children') to travel without them. Yet giving absolute priority to the needs of children is still deep in human nature and is increasingly being enforced by law. That the teaching and example of Jesus give such strong support to this instinctive 'generational covenant' is a point which could have a timely influence on all those prepared to attend to it. But the Working Party made disappointingly little of it.

Yet it would be unjust to say that the Working Party laboured in vain. The greater part of its conclusions and recommendations were eminently sensible, and gave impressive evidence (to those disposed to read it) of a high degree of caring and compassionate understanding among church people towards the most obvious victims of the rapid social changes that have overtaken family life. The question is whether their theological cargo was of any real help to them in their task. Certain things needed to be said, and said with conviction; and in many cases the Christian faith of the authors of the report added precisely that element of conviction which (as we saw in the case of *Faith in the City*) made their work something other, and more persuasive, than an academic study. But the grounds on which their conclusions were reached did not need to be dressed up as 'theological'. Take, for instance, the institution of marriage itself. Statistics show that in Britain it is on the decline, in the sense that an increasing number of couples opt for cohabitation before, or instead of, getting married. Christians instinctively feel that marriage is the superior, indeed the only right, option. But does the fact that this is taken for granted in the Bible and in Christian traditional theology (social changes never until now having caused it to be challenged) give adequate grounds for presenting it as a positive obligation resting on all citizens of the country? In early times Christianity seemed to be making a radical contribution to social mores in giving equal honour to celibacy (a view which is not found in the Jewish tradition). Jesus himself welcomed prostitutes into his company, not necessarily approving their way of life (indeed normally expecting repentance) but nevertheless not making 'respectability' a condition for approaching him. Might it not be at least as 'Christian' to be open to new forms of 'institutional intimacy' as to adhere to the one traditional form at the risk of appearing to censure those who choose another way? And what of the traditional two-parent family? Anyone who has taught in a British school today knows how vital it is to be sensitive to those children who are being brought up by a single parent: if 'family values' are to be taught (as they must be) it is impossible to start with the assumption that only one pattern can be approved of. It is not just common sense but principles of compassion and understanding that are at the heart of Christian discipleship, which compel some qualification to the bald statement that 'marriage is the will of God for the human race'.

Given, then, that marriage cannot now be presented to the world as a 'command' of God (nor indeed ever could have been: celibacy has always been a valid option for Christians, and failure to get married has rightly been regarded as a misfortune, not a sin), how is it to be commended? Certainly Christians may bring to the question their distinctive understanding of the marriage partnership as a 'covenanted' relationship involving a self-sacrificial commitment by each of the parties. But the recommendation to 'society' at large that as many as possible should contract a marriage can hardly be claimed to rest on 'theological' grounds. All that can be said with any assurance is that history, anthropology and sociology offer clear evidence that virtually every known civilization has been built around the institution, and that the risks of letting go of it cannot be known for many generations. The good of society, therefore, seems to demand the prudent course, which is so far as possible to strengthen rather than weaken it. Similarly with extra-marital and pre-marital sex, there is no clear theological basis for its prohibition (and indeed pre-marital intercourse, to make sure the girl will become pregnant, has been customary in many societies even in strongly Roman Catholic countries). If the churches are to continue to insist on abstinence before and outside marriage, they will be wiser to rely on the evidence (such as it is) for the greater permanence of relationships which have been exclusive rather than preceded or accompanied by experimentation with other parties. In default of this, they need to do some hard thinking about the nature of human beings in their sexual aspect and the implications of this for sexual mores. And in this, to date, they have been left behind by philosophers.

One further point may be made before we leave this subject. Homosexual 'marriages', we have said, will soon be coming over the horizon, and it is an urgent matter for churches to make up their minds about them. How are they to do so? It does not look as if 'theology' can be much help. At the same time, the way the question is usually presented is in terms of the 'right' of homosexual couples to receive the same kind of endorsement and strengthening through a public commitment as is given by the marriage ceremony. Put like this, many find the argument hard to resist. Yet there remains a feeling of unease: can the word 'marriage' really be stretched to cover this relationship? Is there not something more at stake than satisfying the 'right' of certain individuals? We shall look at this question in more detail later on in the context of a discussion of human rights. But for the present it can stand as an example of one thesis which is being argued for in this book, namely, that our discussion of such matters is gravely weakened if we approach it in purely individualistic terms. Marriage is a social as well as a personal institution, and the good of society is a primary, not a secondary, consideration. Rights (we shall argue) must be understood (as the first philosophers to discuss them always saw) as closely related to responsibilities, and both rights and responsibilities to an understanding of human beings in their social as well as their individual dimension. 'Theology' may make a return to the scene after all; but it will be doing so, not as prescribing a particular pattern of behaviour on the basis of specific biblical texts, but as promoting an understanding of human nature which is robust enough to provide a criterion by which the alleged 'rights' of individuals can be assessed. The Christian religion clearly demands that we should attend to the aspirations of homosexuals as of any minority group; but the test will be how far those aspirations contribute to a common social good. Theology will do its service so long as its sphere is clearly discerned.

5

Human rights

If there is any moral principle which can be said to have virtually universal support today it is that of the inviolability of human rights. Any instance of apparent discrimination on grounds of sex, race, colour, class (and even, more recently, age) – that is, on grounds of any condition for which a person is not responsible – is greeted with instant and widespread indignation, especially among young people; and the enforcement of human rights through international courts and their monitoring by international agencies – all symbolized and promoted by the creation of a United Nations Commissioner for Human Rights in 1993 – is now taken for granted by most of the international community as a matter of high priority and as a sign of maturing civilization.

It is no wonder, then, that in recent years the churches have added their voices to this chorus; and there have been numerous attempts to ground their support for human rights in Christian theology. Not that this is expected to be difficult: the aims and motivations of human rights movements seem on the face of it to be profoundly in accord with Christian principles (particularly that of the protection of the weak from exploitation and oppression by the strong) and most Christian people probably simply assume that they are a natural extension of the gospel message. But when the matter is looked into more closely difficulties begin to appear, and support for human rights in Scripture and tradition appears less readily available than might have been expected. We need to devote a little time to seeing why this is so.

Do they exist?

There is, first, the basic philosophical question (seldom addressed by theologians) whether human rights exist at all. A positivist would argue that 'rights' of any kind exist only by virtue of laws which have created them: if no law is in place to legitimate my claim to own my own property, then it makes no sense to say that I have a 'right' to it. In fact, of course, most 'rights' that we do claim in our personal lives are so protected; but 'human rights' are by definition ones which apply universally, regardless of whether laws are in place to protect them or not. Those who wish to promote the universal observance of human rights need to begin by finding a philosophical basis for their conviction that such rights actually belong to all human beings *as such*. The Ancient World, for example, though exceedingly sophisticated philosophically, never reached such a conclusion: slaves (and sometimes certain foreigners) were not thought by Aristotle to deserve the same respect as fellow citizens, and women were certainly not accorded the 'rights' which are now regarded as an essential element of any 'human rights' regime – and remained without certain rights, such as that to cast a vote, until quite recently. It was to be many centuries before the concept gained ground that any person whatever had certain rights simply by virtue of being human. When it did so, it was largely by virtue of a philosophical tradition beginning in the seventeenth century with Grotius and Locke, and achieving more general recognition through political writers such as Thomas Paine and through the popular movements which culminated in the declarations of human rights proceeding from the French and American Revolutions. But it is seldom that any philosophical conclusion can be regarded as totally secure. Jeremy Bentham's famous attack on the very notion of human rights as 'nonsense on stilts' has had many followers, and it would be unwise to assume that, simply because they are popular, they will continue to enjoy the measure of support which they receive at present.

If philosophy provides an uncertain basis for human rights, what of theology? When the UN Declaration of Human Rights was drafted in 1948, its inspiration was predominantly Christian and its cultural background transparently Western and liberal. At that time the United Nations Organization (as it was then called) had little more than fifty member states. There are now three times as many, representing a far greater range of religious and cultural traditions. It might have been expected, therefore, that the Declaration would have had to be redrafted to accommodate the greatly increased variety of assumptions that members would bring to the project. In fact, however, the Declaration has stood its ground. Major religious traditions other than Christianity and Judaism have expressed their endorsement, and few have explicitly challenged it. Not that it enjoys unequivocal support from all parts of the world. During the cold war (and still in the eyes of China and some extreme left-wing states) it tended to be suspect as a propaganda instrument for the use of the Western powers; and its interpretation is still liable to give rise to drastically different perceptions of the duties of states towards their citizens. But so far as the great religions are concerned there have been few voices raised against its principles and much support for its promotion as an instrument of international justice and peace. Does this mean that theology (Christian or other) provides a firmer basis than philosophy?

So far as Christianity is concerned, the story is by no means a consistent one. 'Human rights' is a concept that has appeared on the theological scene only recently – and that for good reason. In Antiquity, the idea of a 'right' was strictly connected with law: human beings had 'rights' only by virtue of the general 'right' or 'justice' that states had the responsibility of maintaining. A right, that is to say, was a matter governing the relationship between parties under the law; it could not be claimed by an individual as 'my' right. If this was the case under Roman law, the Hebrew tradition was even less hospitable to the idea of 'human rights'. The Hebrew Scriptures offer a code, not of 'rights', but of obligations – obligations, first, towards God, and then, second, towards fellow citizens. These were not seen as entailing 'rights'. A simple illustration is the humane provision in Deuteronomy that the farmer should not gather his mown corn right up to the edge of his fields but should leave something for the poor gleaners. This expressed something of the social obligation borne by any landed member of society towards the landless poor. But notice that it did not confer any rights on the gleaners. They could not claim entry to the field as of right: it was merely the farmer's obligation to give them access and to ensure there was something for them. If he failed to do so there was no way in which the prospective gleaner could claim redress.

On the face of it the New Testament offers even less scope for a charter of human rights. It has little to say about the law as a guarantee of justice between human beings (though much about it as a factor in their relationship with God), and the teaching of Jesus is at its most radical and challenging when it recommends us to *refuse* to claim our rights, *not* to exact what is due to us and to *allow* ourselves to suffer wrong; moreover St Paul seems to apply this explicitly to any form of legal redress when he asks (even if somewhat rhetorically) why we do not actually prefer to suffer injustice rather than to go to law with a fellow Christian (1 Cor. 6.6–7). There seems, that is to say, to be a principle of non-resistance and selflessness which goes against the very notion of claiming a 'right' for oneself.

On the other hand, this does not necessarily preclude the obligation to claim a right for *someone else*. Indeed it is here that Christianity (alongside Judaism) finds the real reason for supporting human rights. These are essentially a means by which the poor are protected from the rich, the weak from the strong, the oppressed from their oppressors. In the words of Mary Robinson, the former UN Commissioner for Human Rights, 'Human rights law is there because domestic protection of vulnerable individuals or groups is either absent or insufficient' (Romanes Lecture, Oxford 1997). This purpose is self-evidently one to which both Jews and Christians are committed by the many exhortations in the Bible to give protection to 'the poor, the fatherless and the widow' – that is, the most marginalized in any society – and is indeed seen to be inherent in the justice of God himself. It is a concern that has been a high priority for religious people throughout the history of both faiths. What is new is its formulation in terms of 'human rights'; and it is this which we shall need to examine in rather more detail.

The starting point

As we have seen, the language of 'human rights' is something of a newcomer in our civilization. The concept became current in secular thought only in the eighteenth century, and its association with revolutionary activity in France made it highly suspect to the Roman Catholic Church, which felt unable to endorse the values of the French Revolution (liberty, equality, fraternity) until very recent times and therefore gave little theological attention to the 'rights' which these expressed. Protestant churches also, though not necessarily for the same reasons, were slow to embrace the concept of human rights, which, after all, does not appear as such in the Bible and could be regarded as leading people away from the fundamental Christian call to self-sacrifice and loving service. Moreover the idea, though much canvassed in the late eighteenth century, became of less urgency and was little discussed for the next century and a half, and it was only the atrocities of the Nazi period, and the determination of the civilized world to do everything possible to avoid a repetition of them, that caused the concept to be revived at the end of the Second World War and resulted in 1948 in the Universal Declaration of Human Rights. It was this new consensus around what appeared to be a universally shared aspiration which finally impelled the churches to work out their own response to it.

Given that 'rights' language is strange both to the Bible and to Christian tradition, it was necessary to find a starting point elsewhere. A clue was to be found in the word 'universal', which was fundamental to all human rights discourse. Here, it seemed by general agreement, was something which inheres *universally* in every human being. What, then, do all human beings have in common which assures them of these 'rights'? In the religious tradition of Judaism, Christianity and also Islam, what they have in common, without exception, is that they are all descendants (figuratively if not literally) of Adam and Eve, who were created 'in the image of God'. If so, then they – that is, every human being without distinction – are of infinite worth and dignity; and from this it must be possible to reason that they possess 'inalienable rights'. Accordingly, virtually every church statement on the subject begins with the proposition of human beings created in the image of God, and attempts to argue from that to a doctrine of human rights.

It is at this point that the argument becomes slippery. Take, for example, its presentation in the document we have looked at already from another perspective, *The Common Good*. Here the premise is clearly stated: human rights 'derive from the nature of the human person made in the image of God, and are therefore in no way dependent for their existence on recognition by the state by way of public legislation' (§36). This is a clear repudiation of positivism: human rights are *pre-legal*, a given reality that follows from human beings' innate dignity as created in God's image. In the words of Pope John XXIII (*Pacem in Terris*, §9, the first papal encyclical to deal specifically with human rights), 'every human being is a person . . . precisely because he is a person he has rights and obligations flowing directly and simultaneously from his very nature'. Hence these rights are unquestionably 'universal' (§37). It is then said (and this is where the argument becomes tenuous) that these rights 'all flow from the one fundamental right: the right to life' (§37). In order to give substance to this 'right', appeal is made to a further principle said to derive from Roman Catholic teaching, that 'it is the destiny and duty of each human being to become more fully human'. A right to life can therefore be interpreted as the right to those conditions which make this destiny and duty possible, and a list of such 'rights' follows, such as those to religious liberty, decent work, housing, health care and so forth.

The introduction of this allegedly Christian principle (that every human being should become 'fully human') raises serious theological questions in itself. It is often said that it is in Christ that we discover our true human nature; and it is hard to see that Christ required any of these things (decent housing, religious liberty, etc.) in order to achieve his perfect humanity – indeed he was denied most of the 'rights' to which we lay claim, including even that to life itself. Moreover it is surely good 'catholic teaching' (as well as generally acknowledged Christian experience) that a person deprived of the good things of life and reduced to poverty and indignity may manifest a purer humanity than someone more blessed with material advantages. But apart from this, the argument that the right to life necessarily implies these particular 'rights' is itself open to question. The nature of these 'rights' was spelled out in *Pacem in Terris*: they are 'the means which are suitable for the proper development of life . . . food, clothing, shelter, rest, medical care, and finally the necessary social services' (§18). All these things are certainly highly desirable, and there is a clear Christian duty to work for their impartial provision. But to call them 'rights' is to imply that deprivation of them is in some way *justiciable*. In some cases, of course, this may be so: the European Convention on Human Rights (now incorporated in British domestic law) enables a citizen of the relevant countries to claim redress if, for example, employment has been denied on grounds of racial or gender discrimination. But decent housing, social services etc. are in a different category. They may properly be demanded by the electorate, but a government cannot provide them beyond what the resources of the country will bear, nor can it assume that the level of taxation required to fulfil all such demands will be generally acceptable. The concept of 'right' is clearly being stretched to encompass matters which could never be subject to a genuine legal claim.

This stretching of the concept of human rights is characteristic of a great deal of human rights discourse and is at the heart of much confusion. Human rights are said to be 'universal, indivisible, interdependent and interrelated' (*Vienna Declaration*, 1993). They are 'inalienable' and 'inherent' (*Universal Declaration of Human Rights*, 1948). A few of them, certainly, may qualify for these grand attributes: the right not to be tortured, the right not to be imprisoned without charge and the right to life when proved innocent are apparently absolute (though the *Universal Declaration of Human Rights* makes provision for states to derogate even from these obligations in cases of emergency). But the range of 'human rights' now extends far beyond these basic principles. There are economic and social rights; there is even a 'right to development'; and all come under the same description of 'inalienable' or 'universal' rights, regardless of whether any institutions or services are in place which could satisfy them. This forces the question upon us whether it makes any sense to talk of 'rights' (such as the right to employment or to 'a worthy standard of living', *Pacem in Terris*, §11) when the resources simply are not present to make such things available to all. And the more the range of human rights is extended into the realms of culture, politics and religion the harder it is to see how everyone, without distinction, can be said to have a claim on these things *by right*.

The problem, in fact, goes deeper. It is not just the 'second (or third) generation' rights that are problematical. Even the few that are usually regarded as absolute turn out to be subject to exceptions or qualifications. We have already noticed that in times of national emergency governments may suspend the right (for example) not to be imprisoned without charge; and even the right not to be tortured can be difficult to defend in certain cases. If a person holds information that would enable the forces of law and order to rescue a group of endangered people, is not some degree of coercion permissible in order to save innocent lives? If so, how much? And who is to say when it amounts to torture? As for the 'right to life' itself, how can it be formulated so as to take account of the possibility of justified killing in self-defence, of properly authorized military action resulting in deliberately inflicted enemy casualties, and even of the enforcement of law through the death penalty (still not officially outlawed by that same Roman Catholic Church that appeals to Natural Law as the basis for all human rights)?

When philosophers in the seventeenth century began talking

about the 'rights' of individuals (as opposed to the 'right' – *jus* –
which is upheld by the government and the judiciary) they
always stressed that these rights are correlative to duties: if I
have a right to privacy, you have a duty to respect it. Every right
has a corresponding duty laid upon someone else, and any claim
to rights for myself entails accepting the obligations which are
implied by the rights of others. If, for example, it is maintained
that everyone has the right to liberty, equality and fraternity (as
the French revolutionaries were eager to say), then everyone has
the corresponding duty to respect those rights for others; and it
was precisely their failure to accept that obligation that led to
the popular attack on the governing classes at the time. The
problem with 'human rights' is that they do not rest upon the
same symmetrical relationship between right and duty. If I have
the right, which I share with every human being, not to be
imprisoned without charge, and if I then find myself detained as
an asylum seeker in a prison in this country, my problem is
precisely how to identify the party which has some obligation
towards me. The government of the detaining country has, in
principle, obligations only towards its own citizens; and even if
it recognizes its duty, under the UN Convention for Refugees, to
establish whether I have a well-founded claim for asylum, it
cannot be held to account for imprisoning me in the mean time.
This is perhaps an extreme instance (though one affecting some
hundreds of people at the time of writing in Great Britain); but
the principle applies widely. Those who have obligations
corresponding to the human rights of individuals are not other
individuals but governments, and a government is something of
an abstraction when it comes to identifying the party whose
obligation corresponds to a given right and gives that right its
substance. Human rights exist in a vacuum, not only in the sense
that it may be impossible to satisfy them because the necessary
resources simply do not exist, but also because it may be impossible to establish what obligations correspond to them in each
case and whose responsibility it is to accept them.

This problem is recognized in the papal documents, but it is
significant that the argument at this point shows signs of strain.

Pope John XXIII in *Pacem in Terris* stated roundly (§28) that these rights are 'inseparably connected, in the very person who is their subject, with just as many respective duties', and went on to found this reciprocity on Natural Law'. Here the philosophical basis of 'rights' is clearly seen: they exist (other than when enforced by positive law) by virtue of the fact that others accept a corresponding obligation. But the extremely forced examples the pope gives of this correspondence reveal just how difficult this is to establish in the field of human rights: the right to a decent standard of living corresponds to 'the duty of living it becomingly', the 'right to investigate the truth freely with the duty of seeking it ever more completely and profoundly' (§29). Far from being reciprocal obligations towards others implied by those others' rights, these duties turn out to be obligations to no one in particular except oneself (or God), and to be capable of very wide interpretation indeed (what counts and does not count as 'living becomingly'?). These instances certainly do not amount to an argument for the existence of human rights as symmetrically related to social obligations. When *The Common Good* proclaims that 'Every member of the community has a duty to the common good in order that the rights of others can be satisfied and their freedoms respected' (§37), there seems no awareness in the text of just how difficult it is to identify that 'duty' in any particular case. Human rights, by their very nature, defy any attempt to place them in a symmetrical relationship with duties.

In its very first article, the Universal Declaration of Human Rights of 1948 states that 'All human beings are born free and equal in dignity and rights . . . and should act towards one another in a spirit of brotherhood'. The presence of the word *should* at the start of the document suggests that obligations will be treated as being just as important as rights (as Pope John XXIII's exposition seems to demand). But out of thirty nine articles only one makes any mention of them (and even then in a very attenuated form); and subsequent instruments making up today's 'Code of Human Rights' omit them almost without exception. It is this emphasis on rights, at the expense of obligations, which has crept into popular consciousness and is often thought to be at the root of much contemporary social malaise and breakdown of law and order. As a result, attempts are made to redress the balance through educational strategies stressing our social duties; and there has recently been an initiative by Hans Küng and others to promulgate a 'Universal Declaration of Human Responsibilities' based on moral principles shared by all the great world religions. But the real problem lies deeper. It is not a question of reminding people of the obligations which follow from 'rights'; for, as we have seen, these obligations cannot easily be identified. Rather, it is necessary to go back to the original argumentation to see how this essential feature of philosophical and political thinking has become submerged by the rhetoric surrounding the otherwise wholly admirable contemporary movements to promote social justice and human dignity under the banner of 'human rights'.

The concept of the human being

The weakness of all these arguments for mutual and social obligations, and indeed for human rights themselves, can be traced back to the original proposition (a theological one) that these rights flow from the nature of human beings as created in the image of God. It is certainly true that if all human beings are in such a close relationship with their Creator and bear his image, to treat any of them without respect is to show disrespect for God himself. And even for a non-believer, the same point is valid: human life, by general agreement, is infinitely precious and its preservation outweighs all other values; it follows (or at least is deemed to follow in contemporary theology) that every human being has an absolute 'right' to life, to respect and to dignity. The difficulty is to move from this statement about rights to a corresponding one about obligations. As we have seen, the Hebrew code saw things the other way round. It depended, not on rights, but on obligations: you shall love the Lord your God, and your neighbour as yourself. And this stemmed from an understanding of the human being as essentially *social*: we are bound to one another in such a necessary and intimate way that it is impossible to speak of any individual without taking into account the social nexus in which that person is held and the obligations which arise from it. The same essentially social concept was held by Aristotle, for whom any definition of a human person was deficient unless it had a 'political', that is social, dimension: humans are 'political animals' in the sense that their very nature can be understood only in relationship with one another. And the same philosophical tradition ensured the preservation of this essentially social understanding of human nature right through the Middle Ages, from which it followed that the good of society is logically prior to that of the individuals composing it (who will of course benefit in their turn from the 'common good' so achieved). 'Right' (*jus*) remained a property of the legal system which bound society together; it did not pertain to the individual as such.

A change came with the Enlightenment. The model that is found in Hobbes, for example, is not that of human beings all in relationship with one another, but of independent men and women whose interests conflict in such a way that the organs of government are required to enable them to live together without damaging one another. This pessimistic view was rejected by Locke and other Christian philosophers, but the individual model had come to stay. 'All men', wrote Locke (*Second Treatise of Government*, §4) 'are naturally in . . . a state of perfect freedom to order their actions, and dispose of their possessions and persons, as they think fit'. He goes on, of course, to speak of the necessary constraints on this freedom (such as surrendering to the state the authority to punish offenders) which make social life possible; but all the political arrangements he describes exist for the sake of individual human beings: the essentially social nature of men and women, as stressed by Aristotle, has disappeared from the argument. Indeed Locke explicitly contradicts it when he goes on to say (§15) that 'all men are naturally in that state [of nature], and remain so, *till by their own consents they make themselves members of some political society*'. The individual has to 'consent', it seems, to be (in this sense) 'political'. His 'nature' is to be untrammelled by any interests other than his own.

Conceived in these entirely individualistic terms, human beings in the 'state of nature' are conscious only of those needs and desires which they wish to satisfy and to the satisfaction of which they believe they have a 'right'. But as soon as they begin to live in society with others, whom they must believe to be, in this respect, entirely equal to themselves, they discover that they cannot enjoy those 'rights' without being prepared to accord them to others. To live in any peaceful and satisfying society, they have to 'do as they would be done by', and hence follows that network of social obligations which are the foundation of any human community. As we have seen, this model works well enough when these obligations hold between individual persons: to each 'right' corresponds an obligation, and no one can presume to possess 'rights' which do not do so. But political developments from the mid-eighteenth century onwards fundamentally altered the argument. Until then, laws had been made by the wealthy and powerful in their own interest and for the protection of their own possessions. Provision for the poor and powerless was a matter of moral obligation laid on the rich and powerful: there was no way in which the poor and the weak could exercise any 'rights'. But with the extension of the franchise beyond the landed and wealthy classes democratic power shifted in favour of the 'have-nots'. These people now had their 'rights' established in law against the depredations of their social superiors; but it was not obvious that they assumed any obligations in return; and, as we have seen, the evolution of human rights has followed a similar pattern: the poor and the weak now have protection from the strong and wealthy in a way they never did before, but their reciprocal obligations do not appear as part of the arrangement. Hence the shift that is widely observed from a culture based on duties and obligations to one which is preoccupied with 'rights', with a consequent loss of social cohesion and responsibility.

It has also been of considerable significance in the development of modern laws and social institutions. It has resulted in what Jonathan Sacks, the Chief Rabbi, has analysed as a 'civic' as opposed to a 'civil' society (*The Politics of Hope*, 1997). Not that these two are mutually exclusive; indeed (as Sacks argues) both are necessary in any civilized state. But the first, which is basically the Hobbesian concept of a society of strangers requiring the institutions of the state to settle their differences, must not be allowed to overwhelm the second, in which the social instincts and aspirations of human beings receive their opportunity and their encouragement. And for the promotion of this second, or civil, society a concept of the human being is required according to which the capacity for relationships is a defining characteristic. Such a concept Sachs finds in the Jewish tradition, with its emphasis on family values and intimate social networks, which can be traced back to Maimonides and, through him, to Aristotle. We shall see later that a comparable concept is available to Christian theologians. Indeed not only Christianity, but Judaism and Islam also, with their shared emphasis on the command to love one's neighbour as oneself and their shared concern for the common good, have the resources in their traditions to formulate a more adequate understanding of the human being which will serve to support not just the necessary and admirable promotion of human rights which has characterized the last half century, but a recovery of that sense of mutual obligation which is an absolute necessity for any genuine community of human beings. It is becoming urgent that they should rise to the challenge.

6

Volunteers and entrepreneurs

We have looked at a number of social and economic issues where the churches have been ready to offer a 'theological' assessment, and we have seen that the grounding of these assessments and proposals in Scripture and tradition has often been less solid than was claimed. But there is a whole area of social and economic activity which on the face of it is touched much more directly by Christian principles but which has received surprisingly little notice or comment from church bodies. This is the so-called 'voluntary sector'.

First, some facts.

– In Britain today, three-quarters of the adult population gives money to charity.

– One million people do voluntary work.

– Ten per cent of all service sector employment is voluntary.

– The turnover from the voluntary sector is nearly 12 billion pounds.

Behind these bare statistics there lies an impressive sum of effort, generosity and dedication, much of it doubtless undertaken by religious people and sponsored by religious bodies. We may properly ask, what have the churches to say about it?

Charity and good works

From one point of view they say a great deal. Just as the Jewish people have been exhorted for many centuries to perform 'good works' – not specifically commanded in the Law but recognized from at least New Testament times as an essential component of the good life – so Christians have found at the heart of their faith the imperative to succour the needy and give to the poor. 'Whoso hath this world's good and seeth his brother have need and shutteth up his compassion from him, how dwelleth the love of God in him?' (1 John 3.17) is only one of the many New Testament texts, along with the parable of the Good Samaritan, which has made Christians conscious of the need to be perpetually alert to the needs of others and to respond to them to the best of their ability.

There is, however, an important difference between the biblical and the modern approaches to the matter. In the many places where Jesus in his teaching commends almsgiving and the assistance of those in need, the object of the charitable act is not so much the relief of the suffering of the other as the good of the donor. 'Give . . . and you will have riches in heaven', is the characteristic message; the consequences for the recipient are seldom mentioned. Generosity and compassion may of course be stimulated by the wretchedness of those in need; but the motive for giving is assumed to be the spiritual gain which it offers to the giver rather than any radical desire to see the lot of the poor ameliorated. The biblical culture did of course set great store by hospitality, and Jesus pressed this to an extreme point. Everyone agreed it was wrong to turn the hungry away from the door; Jesus taught that one should actually go out and look for them. But the modern notion that the need and poverty of others place a call upon all Christians to respond for the sake of greater social justice and the large-scale relief of suffering, though it is the driving force of a great many charities, is foreign to the Bible. When St Paul argues that his churches should show generosity in aiding their fellow Christians in Jerusalem he does not dwell on the misery they might have to endure without it; he speaks rather in terms of the solidarity which needs to exist between the churches and the need to establish an equality in their mutual relationship. When Jesus commends almsgiving he nowhere refers to the social problems which the giver's generosity might alleviate; he concentrates entirely on the benefits to the giver. Even the invitation to the rich enquirer to give away *all* his possessions is prompted by concern for the man's own well-being, not by any thought of the benefit which might come the way of the poor from such a large donation to charity. The picture of Jesus, so popular today, as a prophet of social justice, authorizing political action on behalf of the poor, is hard to substantiate from the Gospels, or indeed from any part of the New Testament or from early Christian teaching.

This is not to say that Christian charitable giving has always been self-regarding, paternalistic or impersonal. The great flood of charitable and philanthropic enterprises which followed in the wake of the Industrial Revolution and which astonished social commentators throughout the nineteenth century was by no means of this character. On the contrary, great emphasis was placed on the need to be assured that beneficence was being directed to constructive ends and that the donor was taking seriously the human needs and personal dignity of the recipient. Yet it remains true that there appears to have been little theological reflection on voluntary and charitable work, despite the importance of it as an expression of Christian commitment. The questions it raises have been attended to far more vigorously by political philosophers and commentators.

Among these, the nature of the altruistic act itself has been intensively discussed. Is it (as utilitarian philosophers would argue) a calculation of long-term self-interest? Do we do good to others in order that, when in need, we may receive the same from them – as much proverbial wisdom would suggest? Are we mainly (as the Christian sources seem to say) concerned for our own rewards in the future life, charitable causes existing primarily to offer us the opportunity to acquire merit by our generosity? Is it even possible that altruism is merely something built into our genes as a means of ensuring their own transmission through human carriers which are concerned with one another's, and not just their own, survival? Or is altruism a basic human instinct, implanted by God (or at least endemic in human nature), to be nurtured and encouraged for the good of all? Why else would people so willingly donate their blood for use in emergency by others? Why do we respond so readily to the parable of the Good Samaritan, recognizing at once that this is indeed a proper way for anyone to behave, even towards a 'foreigner'? Is not the remarkable level of charitable giving and voluntary work in our society, as it is revealed in the figures given at the beginning of this chapter, testimony to a pervasive and undiminished proclivity in human nature, strongly endorsed in the major religious traditions, to come to the aid of those in need?

If these are questions for the philosopher or the psychologist, some of their implications are of considerable significance for politics. If altruism is characteristic of great numbers of those governed, should government leave the responsibility for social welfare primarily to the 'voluntary sector', only stepping in where 'amateur' enterprise is inadequate or inefficient (which tends, more or less, to be the Conservative view)? Or is all this relatively uncoordinated charitable work simply a transitional stage before the state, with its infinitely greater resources, steps in to make a proper job of it (which has tended to be the Socialist attitude)? When a charitable organization tackles some social problem which causes concern, is its ambition to grow into a nation-wide voluntary agency (such as the Hospice Movement of the last few decades, or such as, in part, the Citizens Advice Bureaux or Victim Support have done, albeit with government subvention)? Or should it rather think of itself as identifying a need and blazing a trail for government to follow by full-scale incorporation into the social services? Should public generosity be actively promoted by government (for example, through tax relief on donations) or should it be stimulated by an element of speculative self-interest (through a lottery), so increasing the revenue available to good causes (though possibly at the same time discouraging private giving and so starving some existing charities)? And what is the effect of all this on the social fabric? Is the amassing of great private wealth commendable if it enables individuals to support charitable institutions more generously (as Mrs Thatcher argued in her famous interpretation of the Good Samaritan)? Or is the kind of society for which we should be striving one in which such major charitable enterprises would no longer be required because there was adequate social provision for all?

New partnerships

These questions would seem to strike deep into the heart of Christian giving and voluntary service, and should surely have evoked some guidance from church bodies. But in fact there has been little or no official comment on them, though the fact that so many forms of 'charity' have political implications is now acutely apparent to many charitable organizations. Overseas aid, in particular, raises questions of a political, as well as economic, nature at every turn – we shall look at this later. But from the beginning charitable and voluntary work has been in potential conflict with government ideology and its promoters have had to make hard decisions as they went along; they have had little help from their churches, which have tended to limit themselves to the traditional encouragement of 'almsgiving', leaving it to others to solve the problems which the actual distribution of the money so raised may cause. Even less do they appear to have taken cognizance of new developments in the relationship between the 'voluntary sector' and the twin economic motors of public and private finance. Instead of the 'voluntary sector' being regarded simply as a supplement to the real business of a post-industrial society, and as a means of channelling the generosity and good will mainly (but by no means exclusively) of religious people into useful objects, there are now signs that a sense of partnership is emerging of profound importance for the whole pattern of society. This surely is something in which the churches should have an interest.

In the first place, evidence has been accumulating (and was recognized, for instance, in a United States government publication, *Reinventing Government*, in 1992) that churches and voluntary organizations may deliver services to society better than government can. Not only may the service be cheaper (in 1997 treatment at the Kaleidoscope Project in London for drug abuse cost £3 per day, elsewhere the bill for medically administered drugs alone cost £4), but it can establish a different relationship with the 'client' involving him or her in the solution of the problem and so having a lasting effect on the person rather than just tackling the symptoms of the trouble. Again and again it has been found that voluntary agencies both work on a smaller budget than comparable state agencies and achieve more lasting results.

Once government becomes convinced of the advantages of 'voluntary sector' provision of certain specialized services, it sees the point of supporting them with public money rather than assuming the whole burden of provision itself. This, of course, is nothing new: part-funding by government has helped a large number of charities to do their work. But in the past it has tended to create a client relationship: the charity is dependent for its grant on government (national or local) and government may retrench without warning and leave the charity stranded. The charity's work, that is to say, has to be tailored so as not to exceed the resources provided in any one year by government grant and its own income from supporters. But now suppose (as is increasingly the case) another partner is involved – the 'private sector'. An insurance company may come to see that the work of a voluntary community project on a housing estate can have an influence on the petty crime rate and therefore on its business. It may then be persuaded that it is in its interest to have a financial stake in the work. But the 'voluntary' element in this new partnership, if it is imaginative, may not be content simply with a financial contribution. The project may invite the company personnel to visit and get involved in the community work, so influencing the outlook and aspirations of a number of individuals who would otherwise never have experienced the realities of the situations against which they were offering 'insurance'. The company, too, may respond positively, and second a member of its staff to gain experience and offer cooperation in the community project. At this point the relationship with government may change also. Subvention from public funds is normally channelled through one department, and forms part of that department's budget. But the nature of the voluntary project is such that it may not readily fall into just one category – 'Health' or 'Education' or 'Heritage, Culture and Sport'. So which department should fund it? Can the question be resolved without some unusual crossing of departmental boundaries? May it not be necessary for a civil servant to become more closely acquainted with the work through some form of secondment? In short, once the full economic and social potential of a voluntary enterprise, both economic and social, is seen by both public and private sector administrators, all sorts of consequences may follow which both secure the viability of the project and have a significant effect on many of the individuals and institutions involved.

The agent of this kind of development has come to be called a 'social entrepreneur'. He or she is usually a person of considerable leadership gifts, of imaginative vision and an ability to inspire others to use their own gifts to the full, giving them the freedom they need to do it in their own way. 'Social capital' is prized above financial capital. Rather than waiting for money to be found before starting a project, the initiative is taken by those who believe in it and money tends to follow until in due course it may even become self-supporting. The social entrepreneur both empowers individuals to take hold of their own destiny, using their gifts to their own and others' good, and persuades those with power and wealth (whether of the government, business or charity worlds) of their common interest in seeing the project succeed.

A key word in work of this sort is 'community'. The word has become exceedingly prominent in social comment and analysis, and denotes something which most people instinctively feel that they need but have either lost or are in danger of losing. It has been called 'a warmly persuasive word', but is notoriously difficult to define. It is well summed up in a few words by the Chief Rabbi, Dr Jonathan Sacks: community is 'the place where they know who you are and where they miss you if you are not there' (*Thought for the Day*, Radio 4, 6 March 2000). The following (non-theological) account of community work from *Faith in the City* (p. 284) gives something of the flavour:

> Community work seeks to involve those concerned in purposeful action to change their situation. Community work intervention is *with* rather than *for* people. Its process involves local people being enabled to raise awareness of issues, ensuring that the objectives are defined by the participants in a situation, attempting to understand the forces at work, discerning what can and should be done and by whom, and supporting those who have become committed to these tasks.

It is easy to see that the work of the social entrepreneur is in effect a form of 'community work': among its most notable exponents are those who have enabled community to grow in places where it had totally disintegrated.

The importance of these initiatives has to be seen in a large context. At the beginning of the twenty-first century it is clear that in modern developed economies the welfare provision established (for the most part) after the end of the Second World War is becoming unaffordable. Throughout Western Europe the proportion of those living well beyond retirement age (a third in the middle of the twentieth century, three-quarters by the end of it) is placing an ever heavier burden on those at work; the technology of health care has doubled or even trebled in cost; a level of unemployment of anything up to 10 per cent, once thought morally unacceptable, is now taken for granted as the necessary cost of a steady economy but imposes a high level of taxation on the rest of the population. Without a considerable increase in taxation, which is generally thought to be politically unacceptable, the present standard of provision by government can no longer be sustained. Right-wing thinkers are responding by proposing a drastic dismantling of traditional welfare arrangements and returning to private and voluntary provision; but the experiments of the social entrepreneurs point to the possibility of a partnership between all the sectors which could revive local communities while securing the necessary provision of social welfare.

These trends have caught the attention of economists, social analysts and politicians. But there has been virtually no response from the churches. Given that the best known of all these developments, that at Bromley-by-Bow in East London, is explicitly church-based (though serving a multi-cultural and multi-faith community), and given that the churches clearly have an interest in 'community' of whatever form, it seems surprising that they are not in the forefront of comment and encouragement. Rather similarly (and sometimes as an offshoot of the 'social entrepreneur' culture) there is considerable impetus, and serious government support, behind the movement for 'healthy living centres', which combine conventional medicine with holistic techniques and give an important place to artistic creativity as an agent of healing and health – at Bromley-by-Bow the patient at the clinic may find himself playing the piano or throwing a pot while waiting to see a doctor and may be given a prescription for gardening or for a silkscreening course rather than medicine; at the Withymoor Surgery in Dudley she can read up for herself all available information on her condition or find herself involved in preparations for a Chinese lantern procession around the district – the surgery has in effect become a hub of the community and its activities. Again, the churches clearly have an interest in such radical approaches to health and rehabilitation (they have traditionally had a commitment to minister to the sick) and might have been expected to make a positive and creative contribution. To the disappointment of many practitioners involved in these ventures there has been little sign of it as yet.

Should this contribution be 'theological', and if so, how would a theological comment on these matters proceed? The most obvious point of contact is provided by the word 'community'. This is a concept in which Christians may well feel that they have a stake. From the beginning the conduct of the Christian life has been seen to involve a particular style of personal relationships, resulting in a 'community' or church that is more than a gathering of individuals for certain purposes but manifests something of the inner nature of the faith. Such a community is represented by St Paul's use of the word *koinonia*, for which no true English equivalent exists: neither 'community' (which is too general) nor 'fellowship' (which is too much to do with emotions and bonhomie) does justice to the solidarity which binds Christians together with one another and with Christ. It involves a willingness to subordinate one's own needs and self-esteem to those of others, to venture in mutual care and service far beyond the ordinary call of duty, to respect the inherited weaknesses and inhibitions of those of different backgrounds and to rejoice in their strengths, and to bring all effort and all ambition into the common striving for a 'community' which by its very existence gives glory to God through its identification with the suffering and the resurrection of Christ.

Such an ideal 'community' may indeed be set before Christians as an inspiration for their common effort and ultimate dreams; but what is its relevance to the public debate on the form of community to be promoted by civic enterprise and public policy? That 'community' in some form is a necessity for human beings living in any kind of society with one another is a datum of philosophical and political thought rather than of theology (though theologians somewhat dubiously press the text, 'It is not good that the man should be alone' (Genesis 2.18) into service to support the proposition), and we must examine the philosophical basis of it later on. Theology may indeed provide guidelines on how *Christians* should live together, but is hard put to it to offer prescriptions for the community life of a multi-faith and multi-cultural society. And the same is true of 'health'. Of course Christianity is deeply concerned with health, healing and the conditions for a fulfilling life. The church is entrusted with a ministry inspired and empowered by Jesus' own activity towards the sick in body and mind, and it exercises this (in theory at least) in partnership with all others who devote themselves to these ends. But the church is also concerned with suffering and illness and with the consolation and redemption which the Christian faith can bring to those who suffer. This is the contribution to the alleviation of suffering on which it has most to say and which is most gratefully received, not only by church members, but by many sufferers of little faith; whereas how to prevent sickness and promote 'healthy living' are questions which have no ready answers in the Bible or Christian tradition, and the reticence of the churches in this area is perhaps understandable. A recent report for the General Synod of the Church of England on 'the Ministry of Healing' (*A Time to Heal*, 2000) was notably thin in its statutory 'theological' chapter.

Perhaps, then, it is not so much 'theology' which is required as the well-motivated application of principles of justice and humanitarian concern that are widely accepted outside as well as inside the churches. But applied to what? It seems that the churches continue to publish reports and statements on social and economic issues as if the terms of the question were the same as they were twenty or thirty years ago. We noted earlier on that as recently as 1997 an ecumenical report on 'work' accepted the assumption that *paid* work could and should be made available to all and gave no attention whatever to the signicant 10 per cent of work which is voluntary and unpaid, even though this work is likely to be done in many cases from profoundly Christian motives. Similarly, Christian excursions into the field of economics tend to assume that the world is as it was a few decades ago. Even David Jenkins' careful analysis of the language of capitalism (*Market Whys and Human Wherefores*, 2000), by which he probed the rhetoric of its promise to bring greater prosperity and happiness to all, ended with prescriptions for a more wholesome political and economic environment which took no account of the radically changing nature of economic activity. To be fair, Roman Catholic teaching has shown some sensitivity to modern trends. In *Centesimus Annus* (1991) Pope John Paul II recognized that the traditional Roman Catholic emphasis on the right to property needed reformulation: 'There exists another form of ownership which is becoming no less important than land: *the possession of know-how, technology and skill*'; and in this connection he noted that '*initiative and entrepreneurial ability* becomes increasingly evident and decisive' (p. 32). This emphasis on 'intellectual property' and the importance of entrepreneurial initiatives is a welcome re-interpretation of the 'right to property' in its conventional sense of land and material possessions and chimes in with the style of some of the most recent economic theory. In this way Roman Catholic teaching has been set free from the shackles of a 'theology' of property which goes back to Aquinas and has little relevance to the modern world. But this is an isolated example. For the most part church pronouncements on economic affairs fail to win respect in the professional world of economists and politicians, not because they lack good sense and sound moral judgment but because they show ignorance of some important contemporary trends. As Ronald Preston, one of the most judicious of political theologians, has remarked on many occasions, the churches need to know what they are talking about in these matters before they say anything at all.

7

Indebtedness, stewardship and social justice

One area of economics in which the churches have recently been both vocal and effective is that of Third World debt. Through their missionary and humanitarian work in developing countries they (or at least their leaders, if not all their rank and file) are probably more aware and better informed than many other people of conditions in other parts of the world that have steadily deteriorated owing to the burden of debt – which, as Nelson Mandela said of Africa on his visit to the British Parliament in 1996, 'we can afford neither to pay nor not to pay'. That prosperous nations which claim to provide substantial 'overseas aid' to Third World countries should in fact be receiving at least as much in return by way of interest on debt was something the Christian conscience began to feel was intolerable in the years running up to the Millennium, and the campaign to persuade the great financial institutions to remit these debts inexorably gathered momentum and received the support of millions of people. These supporters might be of no particular religious affiliation but they shared the sense of outrage that what began as a proper obligation to pay interest and eventually repay a debt had become a means by which the poverty of a country was made irremediable and any measures to lessen the burden were obtained only by submission to the dictates of foreign financial institutions – a form of control from abroad which amounted almost to a restoration of colonial status.

Not that the issue was simple. Commerce of any kind depends

on credit; and credit depends on an assumption that debts will be honoured. 'Cancelling' the debts incurred by poor countries was not just a matter of depriving the original lenders of their regular interest on the loans (actual repayment had long ceased to be a likely outcome in most cases); it risked calling into question the credit-worthiness of all such countries in the future: would comparable loans ever be made again if the lending banks had had their hands bitten by such massive remissions? (This was exactly the problem faced by the Jewish scholar Hillel early in the first century CE: if, as the Bible seemed to say, all debts in the Jewish community were to be remitted every seventh year, how was anyone to be persuaded to make a loan in the sixth year? Hillel therefore introduced a provision, which was gratefully accepted, according to which the regular seventh-year cancellation could be circumvented.) There was also the problem of the use which would be made of the funds released by remission. Not all African heads of state, for example, could be trusted not to syphon off the relief into arms imports or even into private accounts. Some internationally agreed regime would be needed in order to monitor the projects and policies to which the newly available money would be applied; and this would demand a high degree of cooperation between Western financial interests and the recipient governments. None of this was going to be easy, and the difficulties have in fact slowed the process down to an extent that has disappointed many of the original campaigners.

But in this case the churches cannot be accused of having been naive or ill-informed. Their leaders have held discussions at a high level with the World Bank and the IMF. The campaign has enlisted the help of expert economists and financiers. The practical difficulties have been understood and confronted. What gave the campaign its power, and enabled it to enlist supporters on an impressive scale who were by no means regular members of the churches, was its appeal to a generally shared sense of justice and humanitarian concern. It had come to seem to millions of people a clear case of an injustice which should be rectified for the immediate relief of unnecessary suffering, and their indignation grew into a popular movement on a scale that those in power could no longer ignore.

It did, however, gain depth and resonance in the minds of religious people by being associated with the Millennium and so recalling the 'Jubilee Year' which is enjoined in the Law of Moses to be observed every fifty years and which was intended to effect the cancellation of all debt. Some indeed went further, and argued that such remission was actually commanded by the Bible and should be insisted on as a Christian duty. But it is highly questionable whether this 'theological' foundation added any strength to the campaign. In the first place, the interpretation of the 'Jubilee' passages in the Hebrew Scriptures is problematical: it is far from certain whether the Jubilee year was ever observed with a literal cancellation of debts, or whether indeed it had any historical existence at all, its importance being that of a symbol rather than that of an actual precedent. In the second place, the failure of the New Testament to make any mention of it must give Christians pause. Some scholars have argued that Jesus' reference to 'the acceptable year of the Lord' (Luke 4.19) is an allusion to the biblical Jubilee, and that he was therefore proclaiming the remission of all debts as a condition of the realization of the Kingdom on earth. But not only is this dubious exegesis; its significance for the matter in hand would also depend on Jesus' proclamation of the Kingdom being regarded as offering a programme for practical action in the world of contemporary politics and economics. In addition to which, the general point is as relevant here as elsewhere that 'debt' in the global financial system today is an utterly different reality from the kind of indebtedness envisaged in the Bible, which had to do primarily with the relations between landlords and tenants or labourers. None of this provides a secure basis for demanding the remission of 'Third World Debt'; still less should Christians jump to the conclusion that the relative success of the campaign is a victory for biblically inspired action. It is wiser to recognize that the power of the 'Jubilee' movement was its ability to appeal to a generally shared sense of injustice and humanitarian concern. It was almost accidental – though for

Christians and Jews this added a religious impetus to their campaign – that it was enriched by the resonances of an apparently close precedent in the Bible. The real strength of the campaign was a very widely shared moral conviction to do with justice and the prevention of avoidable suffering. And this (and not 'theology') is in fact the strongest ground on which any church comment and action in social and economic matters is ever likely to rest.

Stewardship

Christians, of course, are very used to having the Bible quoted to persuade them to give more systematic financial support to their churches through 'stewardship'. The people of Israel were obliged by the law to 'tithe' their income (that is, give away a tenth part of it) for the support of the temple. In the same way, it is said, church members should give a tithe to the church, so exercising responsible 'stewardship' of their personal resources, and this tithe should in fact be a tenth of their disposable income. But if this is 'theology', it must be said that it is a questionable procedure. In the first place, the word 'stewardship' hardly occurs in the Bible (nor can the concept be easily inferred), and when it does it is used either literally (of the duties of a 'steward') or highly figuratively (as of 'stewarding' the grace or the mystery of God, Eph. 3.2, 9). The idea that the Bible commends 'stewardship' of money (or the environment, for that matter) is without foundation. Secondly, the fact that the cult in Jerusalem was supported by a 10 per cent tax on all citizens is of no more relevance to Christians today than the biblical command (not observed by the majority of Jews even when the temple was standing) to go up to Jerusalem for the annual festivals. And thirdly (a point naively overlooked by many clergy) there is no reason why the objects of an individual's charity should be determined by the church: people give, often generously, to a wide range of good causes and there is no possible 'theological' reason why their giving should all be channelled through their local church. For its own financial health, as much as for enlisting support for international relief, the churches would do better to appeal to their members' generosity for the necessary maintenance of vigorous church life than to invoke a spurious biblical model of 'stewardship'.

Liberation theology

The danger of pressing theology into the service of social concern receives a different kind of illustration if we change our perspective from that of Western Europe to that of Latin America. In many countries in that continent there has been a huge concentration of wealth in the hands of a small ruling class, the mass of the population has remained impoverished and the government has been in the power of right-wing groups or dictators. Political movements to the left have been strongly and at times forcibly restrained by the United States on the suspicion of fostering 'communism', and on occasion have been forced to resort to insurrection and civil war; and in any case democratic institutions have been hard to establish against the force of self-interest exerted by those who have money and power. Meanwhile the indebtedness of these countries to foreign banks has made them necessarily subservient to the policies and constant monitoring of international financial institutions, and in many cases they have obediently invited foreign investment and succeeded in promoting industrialization, increasing exports and stabilizing the economy. But the wealth created by these developments has for the most part merely increased the prosperity of the wealthy classes and enriched the shareholders of the multinationals. The political and economic correctness of their policies has done nothing to remedy a social situation of flagrant injustice – indeed in some cases the poor have actually got poorer in terms of the provision of health care, education and social security: the Western remedies of 'privatization' and 'downsizing' have been adopted in the interests of reducing the taxation of the rich to the detriment of even the minimal services available to the poor.

All this amounts to a situation of flagrant social injustice. Traditionally, the Roman Catholic Church has allied itself with the governing classes, and evangelical churches, frequently originating in and supported by the United States, have tended to do the same. But a powerfully critical movement in the churches, stimulated by the personal dedication of a number of extremely popular liberation theologians, has taken root in many parts of South and Central America and caused the church to be seen as an opponent of right-wing regimes, even to the point of incurring persecution and martyrdom. In El Salvador, for example, the church is acknowledged to have had an 'awakening' (*despertar*) which has both followed and been followed by the murder of a number of priests, missionaries and lay people. The most prominent of these, Archbishop Oscar Romero, is already regarded as a saint in many parts of Latin America – the first archbishop since Thomas à Becket to have been assassinated while saying Mass, and, like him, at the instigation of the ruling power.

The *theological* basis of this movement, as its name suggests, is the concept of 'liberation'. The mass of the people in these countries is truly oppressed by economic and political structures over which they have no control and which perpetuate their poverty and powerlessness. Drawing heavily on the narrative of the Exodus, with its message of divine action to free God's people from enslavement, and combining this with the Christian proclamation of the dignity of every human being created in the image of God, these theologians have promoted a process of 'conscientization' which is nothing other than the encouragement of poor people to take hold of their own destiny and struggle for their 'liberation', inspired by a reading of Scripture which makes people like themselves, rather than the rich and powerful, the focus of God's saving activity. This perspective on the Bible, as we saw earlier, has considerable validity. When read from the vantage point of the poor, many passages come alive with great immediacy; and it is certainly true that one of the most distinctive features of the teaching of Jesus is that it is so often addressed to the very poor, allowing to them a dignity and responsibility for moral action in a way that is strange to virtually all other traditions of moral and religious teaching.

It is no wonder that this movement attracted the suspicion of those in power, who naturally feared it would lead to violent insurrection. In this, for the most part, they were wrong: liberation theology did not encourage violent action unless as a very last resort. Non-violence, forgiveness and reconciliation remained firmly established as the church's characteristic style of action, even in the face of persecution and occasional martyrdom. But there were also serious intellectual objections made from inside as well as outside the church. Liberation theologians made no secret of the fact that they had learnt some of their language and procedures from Karl Marx. Their analysis of 'structural violence' as an inevitable feature of capitalist society, creating inexorable oppression for the poor, owed much to Marxist philosophy; their conviction of the necessity and indeed possibility of radical social change shared the Marxist view of history as moving towards a qualitatively new era; and their emphasis on 'liberation' as a key biblical and religious concept had the same utopian weakness as Marx's projection of post-revolutionary society. A great deal was said about what the poor should be liberated *from*, but little about what they would be liberated *to*: one searches in vain for any serious articulation of the political state of affairs which will succeed when the present oppressive regimes have come to an end. Above all they shared Marx's conviction that the purpose of philosophy (and so of theology) was not to reflect on reality but to change it; consequently the justice and necessity of practical action is given pride of place as a criterion of truth at times even in preference to the dictates of revealed religion.

This explicit alliance with Marxist principles – and indeed with social techniques: the 'base communities', as a means for the 'conscientization' of poor people, bear a striking resemblance to communist 'cells' – inevitably created strong opposition in more conservative parts of the church. The charge most easily levelled against the liberation theologians was that they were wedded to a philosophy which is inherently atheist and could therefore not claim to be genuine Christian believers. This, of course, did not follow: Marx's repudiation of religion stemmed more from his analysis of its social and historical effects than from a serious engagement with its tenets, and in any case the evident faith and commitment of many liberation theologians, leading in some cases to martyrdom, gave the lie to any suggestion that they had exchanged Christianity for dialectical materialism. But the charge that they had too uncritically accepted the inevitability of the class struggle, that their programme for liberating action was more ideological than theological, and that they shared with communism a utopian view of the future that was true neither to historical realities nor to any Christian understanding of the future intended by God, was not so easily met and is still unresolved.

In any case this 'theology' was not what provided the real rallying cry for action. The passionate preaching and fearless social witness of church leaders and theologians in Latin America was a consequence of their sense of outrage at the sufferings being inflicted on the poor and of their solidarity with them. The appeal, again and again, was for 'justice'. The great majority of the population of these countries were being denied their basic rights of property, citizenship and social welfare. They had become, in Oscar Romero's phrase, 'the voiceless', and it was for the church to give them a voice and empower them to overcome the extreme injustices they were suffering. In these circumstances, 'justice' had become a prime Christian priority: the monument to some Jesuit priests who were martyred in San Salvador describes their vocation as being 'for justice and faith' – in that order. It would hardly be possible to claim that this was a top *theological* priority: 'justice' (in this sense) does not have a high profile in the New Testament. But as a motive to command the moral energy of a great mass of people it had and still has great power.

In Latin America this energy is directed mainly at the government of each country, trying to arouse the conscience of the wealthy and powerful and to effect change by political means. But it also arouses strong criticism from the international financial regime. The hold of the World Bank and the IMF over the economies of these countries, and the power of international

business interests, allow little scope even to a socialist government to bring about significant change in the living conditions of
the poor. It is not a 'theology' of wealth, or of business, that is
required to mobilize Christian people to protest against the
shortcomings of the world free market economy. It is simply the
sense of profound and structural injustice which these institutions tend to perpetuate rather than alleviate. Those who
demonstrate against the capitalist system in Seattle or Prague,
whether or not they are Christians, are moved primarily by this
sense of injustice and the need to bring the needs of the world's
poor to the forefront of financial policy. True, this moral
impetus may now be beginning to coincide with enlightened self-
interest. As Mrs Brundtland (formerly Prime Minister of
Norway and now head of the World Health Organization)
pointed out in her Reith Lecture (Radio 4, 3 May 2000), invest-
ing in the health of developing countries is now the only way
that the rich northern hemisphere can protect itself from the
global spread of fatal infectious diseases. As so often, long-term
prudence may be found supporting an immediate moral imperative. But the real spring of feeling and action, both here and in
the poorest parts of the world, is the cry for justice; and this,
more than any 'theology', is the basis of the Christian commitment to respond.

The humanitarian response

But there is of course more than one way of responding to the
misery endured by those who are the victims of economic
oppression. Close to traditional forms of Christian charitable
action are the many organizations working to bring 'humanitarian aid' to places of extreme poverty and deprivation. By no
means all of these have a religious basis; and their support comes
from countless donors who profess no religious allegiance but
whose conscience or sympathy is aroused by the images of
suffering they see in the media. Much of this suffering is known
to be a side effect of economic prosperity in developed countries,

and there are many who are willing to campaign for a more humane face of global capitalism and to make personal sacrifices to this end. But the primary object of their concern and their giving is the immediate relief of suffering, along with support for projects which promote the longer term development of sustainable agriculture, clean water, health and education. 'Humanitarian aid' in this form has become a feature of the international scene and secures remarkably generous support from the populations of the developed countries.

Christian agencies which are engaged in this work confer with each other from time to time in order to establish the rationale of their work and check it against their theological principles. They are, after all, by no means alone in the field. Indeed it is sometimes said that they are simply 'Oxfam with hymns', doing precisely the same work as other agencies that have no religious pretensions at all. Yet their professed motivation is Christian, and they naturally like to believe that they have a style of work which distinguishes them from their secular equivalents. They therefore look for a 'theology' that will undergird the humanitarian (and sometimes political) work to which they are committed. This they have not found easy. They can of course simply say that they are fulfilling the Christian command to love one's neighbour, the neighbour being now just as much in another continent as down the road at home. But this is hardly sufficient to create a distinctive style of action. One concept which has seemed to offer suggestive theological possibilities is that of *diakonia*. 'Service' is a prominent image in the New Testament for the relationship of Christians with one another and with the rest of the world: might it not serve as a model for the kind of work which the Western churches are trying to accomplish for their destitute brothers and sisters in other places? The difficulty is, of course, that the circumstances in which Christians in the time of the New Testament were invited or impelled to 'serve' one another and others were totally different from those of aid workers in distant countries today. How to separate aid from power, how to administer it without creating dependency or offending dignity, how far to engage in political action to promote structural change and tackle the root causes of poverty – such questions would have been totally strange to the world of the Bible, and it is not surprising that no clear 'theology' has emerged. Similarly with the principle, greatly exploited in some ecumenical studies, that the churches must identify themselves unequivocally with the poor and make some redress for the inequalities between north and south an absolute priority: the theoretical support for this very understandable gut feeling shared by many aid workers is to be found more in a somewhat Marxist analysis of economic conditions than in Christian Scripture and tradition. Here I may quote Michael Taylor, a former director of Christian Aid, who has devoted a thorough study to these ecumenical ventures (*Not Angels but Agencies*, 1995). With regard to efforts to define *diakonia*, for example, he writes that 'it is fairly easy to demonstrate that the explicit relationship between them and Christian insights is rather weak' (p. 117). He is even prepared to say that in aid work in general 'the Christian faith has not made too much of a difference' (p. 124). But he does of course immediately qualify this by speaking, very properly, of the influence of Christianity in

> forming Christians to be certain kinds of people who then think and behave, almost without knowing what they do, as the people they have become . . . they grow into the mind of Christ, and it is that 'mind' rather than a great deal of conscious reasoning which makes all the difference. (p. 124)

A 'theology' of humanitarian aid remains elusive; but the motivation of religious people undertaking this and many other forms of social work remains crucial. To this we must return; in the mean time we have seen illustrations of the fact that social action and humanitarian work arise again and again from a profound concern for justice and a deep human instinct to alleviate suffering. 'Theology', at the end of the day, has less importance. It may even obscure the issue.

8

Civil Society

Conservatives and socialists

What sort of society is in the minds of those who are working for political or economic change? How far do the churches endorse any of these programmes or seek to correct them by reference to their own? In due course we must look at specifically Christian visions of society as providing a stimulus to the churches' comments on social affairs. But first let us look at the assumptions which underlie most public thinking about the shape of our society.

We have noted already the view (usually associated with right wing politics) that government in recent years has intervened too much in the affairs of ordinary citizens, and should now be more rigorously restricted to those areas where its services and control are absolutely necessary (mainly defence, law and order and a minimum of support for health, education and social security). The rationale for this finds its simplest expression in the Conservative doctrine that the individual is the person best able to decide how his or her own money should be spent; high taxation for government services should therefore be reduced, allowing the citizen maximum 'freedom' over the disposition of personal wealth. Part of the driving force behind this view is a repugnance to 'dependency': the more the state assumes responsibility for the provison of services to the public, the more the public comes to rely on these services at the same time as complaining about the level of taxation they require; and those who cannot or will not support themselves become 'dependent' on state benefits, to the detriment of their own will to work for their living and of the public purse which becomes stretched beyond the point that is acceptable to the majority. The remedy, according to the simplest form of this view, is simply to reduce the scale of the government's responsibility for the personal well-being of the citizens.

In essence, this is an approach to the theory of government which goes back at least to Hobbes. The nation is thought of as a collection of individual men and women whose interests necessarily conflict and who require a government which will adjudicate between them and enforce the necessary order on their affairs. Whether or not their personal conduct is virtuous and altruistic will depend on their private religious and moral beliefs – and indeed it is characteristic of politicians who take this view that they instinctively appeal to the churches to provide the 'moral cement' in society, government being responsible only for the order and stability which is required for peaceful coexistence. The assumption is that there are only two agents which need to be taken into account. One is the individual, with his or her own needs and interests, potentially in conflict with those of other fellow citizens; the other is government, which has the responsibility of keeping the peace and reconciling these inherently conflictual elements.

But this view (which underlay Mrs Thatcher's famous dictum that 'there is no such thing as society') totally ignores those more informal, less official but still very powerful associations which in fact are an important part of social life. Members of a society do not live (for the most part) as isolated individuals pursuing their own interests without regard either for the good of others or for their own social well-being. They form innumerable networks of friendship, partnership and mutual cooperation, some totally haphazard and unorganized, some thoroughly structured and publicly established. From golf clubs to political parties, from drama groups to churches, organizations exist which recruit their members from every walk of life and bind them into some sort of commitment to a common objective. Such associations normally have rules. They assume some standard of behaviour among their members and require a certain level of commitment to the objects of the association and to the good of fellow members. Failure to observe these rules commonly leads to exclusion, and a degree of trust and reliability is likely to be a condition of membership. These associations, in other words, both rely on and encourage those moral standards and habits which are essential to the healthy functioning of society at large. Far from being an optional extra for society they form its very backbone and influence its moral character. When people ask (as they often do) for the restoration of conscription to military service in order to 'teach dicipline' to the young, they forget that in the past this was done very effectively by the many uniformed organizations which flourished until the last half century (when they began to decline) – Scouts and Guides, Boys' Brigade, Church Lads' Brigade and many others. And in many other ways it was the voluntary organizations – many of them attached to the churches but by no means coterminous with them – which provided much of the 'moral cement' of society.

If this element in society is largely overlooked by those who follow the Hobbesian model, it is equally undervalued in much socialist thought. Thinkers on the right frequently blame the rise of socialism in Britain in the early part of the twentieth century for the decline of those many voluntary and charitable associations which were such a marked feature of Victorian England. There is undoubtedly some truth in this. The objective of a fair and equal society, which is a driving force in socialist thought (however utopian it may seem), implies the need for government action to rectify social injustices, so putting voluntary and charitable enterprises out of a job. Traditionally, socialist governments have been less hospitable to voluntary social work than Conservative ones; yet whether the socialist philosophy has been the true cause of the decline of voluntary social provision is not so obvious. The decline, after all, has continued throughout the twentieth century despite long spells of Conservative government, and may be due to deeper causes. Indeed it is surely related to that individualism which has entered Conservative thinking as much as any other and which is totally different from the conception of civic virtue which animated the widespread philanthropic activity of nineteenth-century England. A culture obsessed with individual rights at the expense of mutual obligations tends to force the presence and importance of voluntary activity out of the sphere of current political vision. Moreover the economic model of government assumes that every individual makes virtually all choices for maximum personal gain and that if 'services' are provided by voluntary agencies this should be done 'under contract' (so forcing charitable work into the uncongenial mould of 'efficient' service provision). Yet, as we have seen, the will to engage in such activity appears to be as strong as ever.

'Civil society'

It is in this context that we should understand the renewed philosophical interest in the concept of 'civil society'. This can plausibly be traced back to Hume and the Scottish moralists of the eighteenth century (by whom 'civil society' was contrasted with the state of 'barbarism' in which every man is out for himself), and rested on the assumption that the functions of government are limited to law and order at home and abroad while the moral and social life of the citizens is maintained by civilized and civilizing institutions springing from a shared concern for the common good. This concept is seen as having borne practical fruit in the nineteenth century, when voluntary philanthropic associations proliferated to an extraordinary degree. Confronted by extremes of social deprivation and misery, concerned individuals did not (for the most part) immediately demand government action in the name of social justice; they roused public opinion to create philanthropic agencies for the relief of the victims. In due course this popular concern was translated into political pressure for legislation in the form of such things as Factory Acts and the political enfranchisement of the poor; but the characteristic form of social action in Victorian England was represented by an astonishing number of non-state 'political' associations, recognized and protected by law, but relying entirely on charitable support and independent of government funding or influence.

During at least the first half of the twentieth century these organizations certainly declined. Whether or not the cause of this was the attitude of the governments of the time, it is certainly true that many of the objects for which they were founded came to be assumed to be the responsibility of the state, and political debate has not seriously challenged the assumption that a just provision of protection for the most vulnerable members of society is a priority for any government. This has been accompanied by a growing emphasis on the 'rights' of the individual citizen, with a corresponding decline in any sense of civic obligation towards others. Those philosophers who are promoting the concept of 'civil society' see the encouragement of voluntary associations as a means of restoring a shared moral consciousness in society. It is true, of course, that in a modern 'pluralist' society, in which every citizen is assumed to have the right to hold his or her own beliefs and values, even the possibility of a shared moral system of values is open to question. But the existence of consensus on certain moral principles, such as the inviolability of fundamental human rights and freedoms, the necessity in any commercial or social enterprise to regard promises as binding, and the undesirability of a growing gap between the richest and the poorest, shows that in practice there is at least an overlapping range of moral principles shared by the great majority of citizens, and these find their most articulate and energizing expression in the activities of voluntary associations set up to work for the amelioration of widely perceived injustices and discriminatory practices. Many schools, for example, take it for granted that some involvement in charitable work should form part of the moral education of their students in order to make them sensitive to the suffering of those less fortunate than themselves.

A significant illustration of the importance of such associations can be seen on the international scene. The United Nations Organisation was created after the Second World War as a community of states committed to the maintenance of peace through negotiation rather than armed conflict. Though its Charter also recognized the protection and promotion of human rights as an integral part of this objective, the purposes of the organization were on the 'Hobbesian' model of a superior authority arbitrating between the conflicting interests of individual states and maintaining law and order among them. It was soon found, however, that the promotion of peace and the prevention of armed conflict demanded more than a fire-brigade reaction to actual conflagrations: only a concerted attempt to tackle the deeper causes of conflict – such as poverty, malnutrition, and unregulated access to the resources of the sea – would make it possible for the UN's overriding purpose to be fulfilled. Hence there rapidly grew up a number of subsidiary organizations and agencies to do with economic development, health, refugees and so forth, which ever since have been doing work which has won the respect even of those who doubt the ability of the UN ever to secure world peace. These agencies, accountable to the UN and funded by member states, are in that sense arms of (international) government, an extension of the remit with which the organization was originally charged and a clear departure from the principles of those who would otherwise argue that the role of government should be strictly limited to the spheres of law and order and international relations. But then there was a further evolution. Recent decades have seen the proliferation of 'non-governmental organizations' (NGOs) which are unofficial, mostly voluntary, and represent the concerns and interests of a great variety of associations. Most of them are international and humanitarian, and are committed to high objectives such as the regulation of the arms trade or the provision of clean water in developing countries. From small beginnings these NGOs have grown into a powerful force in world affairs, such that any major international meeting of politicians and official government experts may find a parallel 'unofficial' meeting taking place simultaneously, which, particularly if the media are sympathetic to their cause, may exercise considerable influence on the policies agreed by the 'official' representatives of the nations. NGOs, that is to say, are the expression of 'civil society' in the international arena, corresponding to the informal associations within any nation which play (at least according to this view) an important part in the life of any society and fulfil a role which it is improper, if not impossible, for governments to play themselves.

The role of religions

Among these voluntary associations, religions have a special place. Others, for the most part, have limited objectives and only partial claims on people's lives and interests. Amnesty International is concerned with victims of unjust imprisonment, Greenpeace with the environment and so on. But religions claim to offer guidance in every aspect of a person's life and even to be able to pass judgment on the conduct of public affairs. The 'Abrahamic' faiths in particular (Christianity, Islam and Judaism) have a deep traditional concern for 'justice' which entitles them (so they would claim) to be vigilant not only about the processes of law but also about the effects of public policy on the weakest and most vulnerable members of society. In this sense they have a comprehensive remit which distinguishes them from other voluntary associations, and which has historically been the cause of much friction and even violence. One religious world-view may conflict with another in certain particulars, and the temptation to use force to impose one over the other has not always been resisted; indeed there are not a few parts of the world where such conflict is still simmering, or even raging, today. But in the West, for the most part, the slow evolution of the liberal values of tolerance and respect for religious freedom has created an environment in which religions are able to flourish in peaceable coexistence, so long as their adherents cause no trouble to other citizens.

This evolution, however, has taken place at the same time as one religion – Christianity – has held a dominant place in society, whether through an 'established' church or simply through its historic influence on the culture and institutions of the nation. The arrival in the United Kingdom (as in other countries of Western Europe) of large numbers of immigrants professing another world religion, along with the increasing 'secularization' of (or decline of religious belief in) society has called this traditional supremacy into question. How should these religions now be related to one another and to the rest of society? One model – the 'Hobbesian' model – results from the simple application of liberal principles. The task of the state is to provide legal protection for each major religion, ensuring the freedom of its members to follow their observances and imposing only the necessary restrictions on their conduct to prevent harm or offence being caused to others. This is one sense which may be given to Prince Charles's suggestion (in connection with the Coronation Oath) that the monarch should become, not 'defender of the faith' but 'defender of faith': the law of the land, of which the Crown is the ultimate guarantor, should provide a secure environment for religious belief and practice, and if any one religion is still dominant its members must respect the freedom of others and restrain any impulse to use their position for proselytizing.

The application of this model has undoubtedly brought great benefits to religious people in many places, and afforded them a greatly valued security in pursuing their own chosen way. But it implies a somewhat negative judgment on the value of these religions themselves. Are they merely troublesome and persistent elements in society requiring regulation and control in the interest of the peace and harmony of society at large? Or do they have a more positive contribution to make, particularly in the moral education and guidance of their own members and even of others? It is here that the model of 'civil society' becomes attractive. The development of interfaith cooperation and understanding has in many places fundamentally changed the relationships of religions to one another and enabled them to discover large areas of common interest and moral consensus. Profound doctrinal differences do of course remain, and may even cause conflict; but the experience of individuals who find themselves neighbours to people of other faiths whom they come to respect, and of faith communities which are confronted by common problems, has brought a new realization that by professing a religion a person may be accepting responsibility for the well-being of others far outside the realm of one particular faith. A striking example is the reaction of churches, mosques and synagogues to the plight of asylum seekers in Britain after the punitive legislation of 1996: members of all three faiths worked together to provide relief and assistance to these extremely disadvantaged people regardless of what religion or culture they belonged to. On this occasion the concern for the outcast and the stranger that is deeply entrenched in all three faiths found expression in shared initiatives and common action. The concept of 'civil society' allows for a positive appreciation of work of this kind: religions are among those voluntary associations – are indeed among the most important of them – which are essential for the well-being of society and which alone can provide the moral education and nurture which will stimulate concern, not just for the individual, but for the good of all – especially for the most vulnerable of our fellow citizens.

Indeed in this new climate of interfaith ecumenism the contribution that can be made by religions may go considerably further than humanitarian social action. They may, for instance, provide significant support for the promotion of human rights. When the Universal Declaration of Human Rights was approved by the members of the United Nations in 1948 it was heavily influenced by the Christian and liberal principles of Western thinkers. Since then over a hundred new states have become members, the majority of them non-Christian and non-Western. But these also have found in their own religious and cultural traditions enough common ground to be able to endorse the principles of the Declaration, and the world religions for the most part have shown significant willingness to throw themselves into movements to support human rights, given their common belief in the inviolable dignity of every human being as created by God. Their failure, as we have seen, is not having tempered their enthusiasm for 'rights' with a more balanced understanding of the essentially social nature of human beings. Similarly, they have a common concern (shared with an increasing number of their fellow citizens) for the environment. Unlike politicians, their leaders can take a long view – even a 'prophetic' view – of social and economic developments. They can, for instance, alert society to the damage which the pursuit of purely 'secular' values (such as those of the free market economy) may cause, and at times propose practical ways of avoiding or reducing it. And the experience of interfaith dialogue itself, which has been slowly and often painfully learnt by those who have taken part in it, may have a contribution to make on a wider stage. It involves patient listening, sensitive speaking and a readiness to subject one's own deepest convictions to reappraisal in the light of the glimpses one obtains of another's faith. It is an experience which, if more widely shared, could have an incalculable influence on the relationships of different groups and interests within 'civil society'.

All of this has some bearing on the question with which we started: on what grounds may churches presume to contribute to the public debate on contemporary moral and social issues and make recommendations? In a country with an established church such as England or Scotland it could be argued that such social comment could be made as of right. The cultural and moral assumptions of the nation have been formed under the influence of Christianity, and it is appropriate that the same tradition should be brought to bear by its most authoritative interpreters (who are presumably the church authorities or experts commissioned by them) on any issues now in dispute. But this Burkeian view of the matter runs counter to the generally perceived reality of Britain today, in which barely 10 per cent of the population actively profess the Christian faith and where almost equal numbers are fervent followers of other religions. Our society, that is to say, is 'pluralist'; and the established norms of a liberal polity give every man and woman the right to their own opinions and make it inappropriate, if not actually immoral, for any one set of moral principles to be imposed by any authority on those who do not hold them. On this view the churches have no right to pontificate to anyone outside their own membership: that they should issue a document such as one entitled 'A Call to the Church and the Nation' is an arrogation to themselves of a high moral ground which they no longer occupy. Churches are entitled to speak only to their own faithful.

A *third way*?

Is there a middle ground between these two views? It is often argued that this is in any case a simplification. Even if it is only a small minority who explicitly call themselves Christians, the influence of Christianity in our culture is pervasive and pertinacious. People continue to choose Christian schools for their children and to ask for Christian ceremonies marking birth, marriage and death in far greater numbers than go regularly to church, and moral judgments based on Christian principles will receive approval far outside the confines of the churches. If church authorities make pronouncements on matters of public concern they can expect to be listened to with respect by far more people than would call themselves professing Christians. To this extent it can be plausibly argued that churches may still address a wider public and even government on a range of issues outside their specifically religious territory and expect to command attention. And certainly it is true that a great many people who are without religious faith but who have been brought up in a recognizably Christian culture will respect authoritative church pronouncements and even expect the churches to 'say something' when serious moral issues are in question. But this somewhat optimistic or conservative view does not take account of the growing number of faithful members of other faiths in this and other European countries who cannot accept, and will naturally resent, the pretensions of the Christian religious authorities to speak to, and even for, the whole nation. The realities of the 'pluralist' society are such that for the churches to speak in this way may seem to others little more than an attempt to maintain their dominance in a society which has in fact become a republic of varied faiths and attitudes. If they speak, they should surely confine themselves to addressing their own members.

The model of 'civil society', however, offers a third way. Once it is established that there is a range of moral principles and issues on which the major religious traditions agree, and that their distinctive contribution to society rests on the fact that their members adhere to these principles and approach these

issues out of deep religious conviction, then the act of giving
these principles and judgments expression in official reports and
pronouncements ceases to be a cause of resentment and becomes
a legitimate form of participation in public debate. When
Christian theologians find themselves members of, say, an
ethical committee set up to monitor procedures in one of the
armed services, or of a working party on the reform of some
aspect of the law, they do not wait for the unlikely event of their
being asked to contribute a specifically Christian view of the
matter; rather they are there to bring the discipline of their moral
thinking and the strength of their moral convictions to bear on
issues where there is already a substantial degree of moral
consensus, the difficulty being to weigh priorities and allow for
conflicting interests in any particular case. Similarly, on the 'civil
society' model, religions have the task not simply of adding one
more voice to the many already competing for a hearing, but of
articulating and giving coherence to a latent moral consensus
which exists far outside their own communities. They may well
find it appropriate to reassure their own faithful that their judgments and recommendations are consistent with their own
religious traditions, their scriptures and their doctrines; hence
they will legitimately do some 'theology' in relation to the issue
in hand. But it will not be on that basis that they commend their
judgment to the general public, but rather as the application of
principles which they share with, or which at least are well
understood by, the majority of their fellow citizens and which
their religious faith allows them to express with particular
conviction and clarity.

A notable example of such action, taken in this case by the
Church of England, is in relation to the laws relating to divorce.
In the years following the Second World War it began to be
realized that the adversarial character of all divorce proceedings
(the law being based on the presumption that one of the parties
to them must be 'at fault') was resulting in much unnecessary
suffering and in some cases in an abuse of the legal system – one
barrister (my father) was even led to argue, in a famous article in
the *Modern Law Review* (C. P. Harvey QC, April 1953, pp.

129–39), that the state of the 'Divorce Market' was such that it would be preferable if at least undefended divorces could be obtained (after appropriate bureaucratic delays) through the Post Office. After two abortive attempts by individual Members of Parliament to have the law changed, the Archbishop of Canterbury appointed a group of experts to study the matter, and its report was subsequently published under the title *Putting Asunder* (1966). It was at least partly under the influence of this report that the law was eventually changed, and the notion of 'matrimonial fault' ceased to be the determinant factor in divorce cases; the question now became whether the marriage had 'irretrievably broken down'.

The interest of this example is that marriage and divorce are matters on which religions certainly have something to say. Christian doctrine is clear on the undesirability of divorce in almost any circumstances, and a Christian contribution to the debate might have been expected to promote any measure that would make a divorce more difficult to obtain. In fact, however, the members of the Church of England working party were moved primarily by practical considerations and moral sentiments which were shared by the great majority of the population, whether Christian or not. They noted the unsatisfactory state of the law as it stood and the suffering caused by the necessity always to apportion blame to one party in a divorce suit and the injustice this often caused either when both parties appeared equally to blame or when factors such as mental illness made the marriage unsustainable. They therefore proposed that irretrievable breakdown of the marriage should take the place of matrimonial offence as the ground for divorce. It was seen at once that this might make divorce 'easier' to obtain (though this was strongly contested by the Archishop's group) and the proposal was resisted by some church members on precisely these grounds. But the proposed change was in due course adopted by the government, and came about to a large extent through the influence of the established church. Significantly, this influence was based, not on distinctively Christian doctrine (which might have produced the opposite conclusion), but on a widely shared

sense of injustice and of the need to alleviate avoidable suffering.
As the group stated in its report,

> Any advice which the Church tenders to the State must rest,
> not upon doctrines that only Christians accept, but upon
> premisses that enjoy wide acknowledgement in the nation as a
> whole . . . [in this case] the only Christian interests that need to
> be declared are the protection of the weak and the strengthen-
> ing of those elements in the law which favour lasting marriage
> and stable family life; and these are ends which Christians are
> by no means alone in thinking socially important. (§§17–18)

A contribution of this kind to public debate fits well into the
concept of 'civil society' as elaborated by political philosophers.
But the concept is by no means confined to philosophy. It has
been strongly argued for by the Chief Rabbi in his book, *The
Politics of Hope* (1997); it is the title of a Muslim periodical
devoted to exploring the Muslim contribution to social and
political questions; and the term has entered the vocabulary of
political leaders as a general designation for all those agencies
and institutions beyond the range of government which
maintain the health and vitality of a democratic society. Such
language is a positive challenge to the churches, along with other
religious bodies, to make their contribution; but they will do so
best, not by seeking to commend a distinctively 'Christian' or
'theological' solution, but rather by lending the weight of their
own convictions and the strengths of their analysis to an ethical
judgment which will command assent from many outside their
own membership. How this affects their authority for addressing these problems at all is a question to which we must return;
but first we must face the challenge presented by those who
would reject any such 'liberal' approach. Surely, they will say,
Christians have a vision of society which is stronger and more
distinctive than this? Is there not a gospel message that society
must be transformed, not simply adjusted, if it is to approach the
standards demanded by the preaching of Jesus? This will be the
subject of our next chapter.

9

Visions of the Kingdom

A radical alternative?

The typical twentieth century phenomenon we have studied so far (which shows every sign of continuing into the twenty-first) is that of Christian people becoming alerted to a particular social problem and addressing it through their representative bodies by means of a study or report which could be entitled 'The Church and . . .' or (in the case of individual theologians) 'The Theology of . . .', the phrase being completed by a subject such as 'work', 'family', 'human rights' or even (as in a recent Church of England report) 'cybernetics' (*Cybernauts Awake!*, 1999). Society, that is to say, sets the agenda; the church responds with a 'Christian' view. But this approach to social and economic affairs strikes some Christians as compromised from the start. Surely it is the church, not society, which should set the agenda? Does not Christianity propose a total vision of society towards which all Christians should be striving and in which particular questions of this kind should find their solution? Is not this piecemeal approach to contemporary issues an abdication of the Christian responsibility to work for a state of affairs radically different from that in which we find ourselves, in which power and self-interest give way to justice, compassion and mutual service – in short, the Kingdom of God?

It was an impulse of this kind, as we saw in Chapter 2, which caused some of the contributors to *Faith in the City* to publish their own understanding of God's 'Kingdom' as offering a more radical analysis of the state of the nation in the light of Christian social thinking (*Theology and Social Concern*, Church

of England Board for Social Responsibility, 1986). The reasons
why their approach was rejected by the majority of the
Commission were pragmatic: they were anxious above all to
make the kind of recommendations which would be sufficiently
realistic and practicable to have some hope of being adopted by
decision-makers in church and state; the plight of those living in
the inner cities and sprawling conurbations of England was too
urgent to allow the luxury of what could appear as utopian
theologizing. But the initiative of those who took the more
radical view deserved serious consideration, and there may have
been better reasons for rejecting it than the pragmatic ones
which prevailed at the time. There is, after all, a subject called
'Political Theology'. Does not this give us a framework in which
to make Christian judgments on matters of public policy?

It could of course be immediately objected that to follow this
line would be to disqualify Christians (let alone churches) from
making a serious contribution to public debate. If the presuppositions they carry into the discussion arise entirely from their
own faith and are ones that are not now shared by the majority
of the population they can hardly expect a respectful hearing.
But this is greatly to simplify a complex question which has
received different answers throughout the history of the church.
Church and state are always in some form of engagement with
each other. In some periods the church has insisted on a separation of spheres of influence, apparently preferring to confine
itself to religious and spiritual matters and leaving practical
decisions to those who have the responsibility for the material
well-being of the nation. In others (particularly in what we know
as 'Christendom') the church has proclaimed an interest in a
substantial area of 'secular' affairs, and in more recent times
there have even (in continental Europe) been 'Christian' political
parties. Those (and there are many) who insist that the church
should 'keep out of politics' need to reflect that for most of its
history the church has been deeply involved in political issues
and is likely to have had plausible reasons for doing so. The
distinction between 'spiritual' or 'religious' and 'practical' matters
is a slippery one; it was not recognized at all in the Bible (so that

many Christians are naturally unwilling to accept it) and is difficult to maintain in the face of the number of practical matters, from divorce to warfare, on which Christians will feel themselves constrained by their faith to adopt a particular position. History does not support the proposition that in public debate on social or economic issues a specifically Christian contribution must be ruled out of court.

Re-introducing God

There is also a more profound reason. Before trying to exclude theology as an intruder on the political scene, it is necessary to ask what authorities are in command there. For all the apparent certainties frequently assumed by politicians – that they are authorized to exercise power by their election according to recognized democratic procedures, that their actions are legitimate because constitutional and so forth – the nature and extent of political power remains a baffling philosophical problem to which no enduring answer has ever been found. What gives one person authority over another, how far any citizen's freedom should be limited by the interests of 'society', whether one person should have an absolute right to more property than another, on what principle the state should influence the free circulation and distribution of goods – these and many other questions remain unsolved. For many centuries in the West it was taken for granted that political authority in some sense derives from God and is legitimated so far as it conforms to the divine will; this was then replaced by a belief that human beings at some moment entered into some form of 'contract' under which they renounced certain individual rights and freedoms in return for the protection of law and superior administration. Since no historical moment was ever proposed – or could have been – when such a contract took place, this explanation of political realities was clearly relying on an explanatory myth rather than on any empirical findings; equally the utilitarian analysis, according to which particular political institutions are acquiesced in because they, rather than any other, can be relied on to provide the greatest benefit and the least disadvantage for all, presupposes that the mass of the population goes in for an elaborate calculation of gains and losses which is clearly beyond the capacity of any but a small elite. Yet such theories continue to underlie the thinking which supports the maintenance or the reform of political arrangements, even in a 'post-modern' age which rejects in principle the possibility of any single agreed philosophy of government. No one could say that the vacuum left by the removal of God as the ultimate authority for political power has been filled by another concept that commands universal agreement. In which case, may it not be appropriate for Christians along with other religious people to propose that God should be reinstated?

There is of course a positivist reply to this. Constitutions are made by human beings: once agreed, they provide the authority required for government to be conducted. Laws are made by a legislative assembly: once passed they apply to every citizen within the state's jurisdiction and determine what is lawful. In international affairs (this was the view of Kant) all law depends on treaties: only when nations have mutually bound themselves to (for example) refrain from attacking each other can it be said to be 'wrong' for one of them to do so. If this is the case, clearly there is no room for religious bodies to appeal to a superior authority or an eternally enduring principle. Political institutions and rules of government are what we make them to be; the role of religions is at most to influence individuals in such a way that they make their decisions in these matters with honesty, prudence and concern for the general good.

Positivism has a strong intellectual appeal. It removes the sense of mystification which seems often to be introduced by philosophers when they try to account for political phenomena by general and abstract principles. It has the advantage of simplicity and pragmatic common sense. It avoids the need to trace the origin of political principles back to religious beliefs or supposed moments of popular consensus. The snag is that this is not, for the most part, what people actually believe. Certainly constitutions are human-made; but their makers were seldom merely consulting their own interests or taking the best from other existing constitutions. More often they were applying general principles of just law and government (as they understood them) to the particular needs of their country. That is to say, they believed that these principles existed independently of their own constitution-making, and were prior to their expression in any particular constitutional formulation. Similarly with human rights. Certainly these are now expressed in legal and constitutional documents in many countries and are formulated in conventions to which states have become formal signatories; but few would take the positivist line that these rights do not exist until they have come on to some statute book: on the contrary, it is because of a shared and general consciousness of the existence of these rights that the conventions and treaties have come into existence. And so, too, with international law itself. When the General Assembly of the UN voted by a large majority to outlaw reprisals as legitimate military tactics, this was not either a deliberate political innovation or a generalisation from the rules of engagement of any particular army. It was the application to international affairs of a moral principle increasingly recognized by member states – just as, in domestic legal procedure, appeal is made to 'natural justice' as a factor which may properly influence a judgment, whether or not it is embodied in any existing law or court ruling. The practice of both national and international courts presupposes the existence of certain legal and moral principles whether or not they are embodied in a written code; and similarly the working of any constitution needs to obey rules and conventions (such as the duty of honest reporting to higher authorities or of a defeated parliamentary minority to respect laws passed by the majority) whether or not these are actually written into the founding document – though subsequent disputes may make it necessary to do so, as in the case of Amendments to the American Constitution. The neat and logical analysis of political institutions offered by positivism runs counter to the actual beliefs and practices of too many people for it to be acceptable as a definitive account.

But where does 'natural justice' – this belief in the rights of the individual, this principle of political propriety – come from? Given the philosophical uncertainties which surround the question, we have to confess that much is mysterious, and it is perfectly legitimate for religious people to propose God as the author and guarantor of right and wrong in the political and legal spheres just as much as in the sphere of personal morality. After all, for the greater part of the last two millennia this has been taken for granted. It was accepted that human justice is always corrigible in the light of the justice of God, that human rulers are accountable to the Ruler of all, and that human subjects owe obedience to the authorities set over them as representatives (so far as human sinfulness and frailty permit) of divine rule over the created order. The decline of a belief in God, coupled with the Enlightenment faith in the power of the human mind to answer these questions without divine aid, started the West on a quest for another source of moral and political authority that could be located in the human will and the human understanding. But the quest has led to no generally accepted solution, and indeed (according to post-modernism) to the conclusion that no such solution is possible. In which case it is not unreasonable to suggest reintroducing God into the argument, particularly if this can now be done on behalf of many world faiths and not just one.

This is the claim argued for in one of the few books of serious political theology that have been written in English in recent years, Oliver O'Donovan's *The Desire of the Nations* (1996). Drawing heavily on the Old Testament, O'Donovan proposes four features of God's 'kingship': salvation (in the sense of providing a purpose for his people and the resources to achieve it); judgment (in the sense of demanding just procedures in legal institutions, with a necessary bias in favour of the poor and the weak); 'possession' (in the sense of a homeland and a cultural continuity assuring the nation's continued identity); and an answering response to this expression of kingship in the form of 'praise' (in the sense of an acknowledgment of the sacredness of the God-given springs of national life). These features are modified and refined in the teaching of Jesus and the witness of the Apostolic Church but remain foundational for our understanding of the way in which God may be said to 'rule' the world and provide the ultimate source of political authority (and also, of course, of authoritative criticism of any particular manifestation of that authority). On this basis, O'Donovan makes an important claim: this analysis, he writes,

> explains, as very few attempts at theorising the foundations of politics ever do explain, the persistent cultural connection between politics and religion. And it allows us to understand why it is precisely at this point that political loyalties can go so badly wrong; for a worship of divine rule which has failed to recollect or understand the divine purpose can only be an idolatrous worship which sanctions an idolatrous politics . . . The doctrine that *we* set up political authority, as a device to secure our own essentially private, local and unpolitical purposes, has left the Western democracies in a state of pervasive moral debilitation, which, from time to time, inevitably throws up idolatrous and authoritarian reactions. (p. 49)

This is a bold claim indeed: if political society departs from an understanding and acknowledgment of its divine authorization it is liable to impoverishment and decline. For the Christian believer this may be a profoundly helpful way of looking at the matter. It explains, for instance, why political terms such as 'kingdom', 'authority', 'power', have been from the beginning integral to the formulation of the Christian faith: they are not used as analogies, as if prior political realities were invoked to illuminate the nature of God's presence in the world; rather they express enduring aspects of God's will for human beings, of which any human institution is a more or less fallible representation; and when societies lose sight of this reality and cease to acknowledge it they are liable to fall into decline. Should Christians therefore seek to impose this understanding of political authority on others, along with those forms of political institution which seem most congruous with it?

Objections

There is a number of reasons why this is not at all what they should do. First, the fact that their theology offers an answer to a question to which no other fully satisfying answer has ever been found (the question of the ultimate source of political authority) is not in itself a compelling reason for others to accept it. In a pluralist society all individuals preserve the right to reject a doctrine based on a faith they do not personally share, even if they have no equally satisfactory doctrine to put in its place. Religious people may wish to commend to others the idea that a belief in God provides the best available explanation of the origin of political authority; but this certainly cannot be used as an argument for imposing on others a particular political system on the grounds that it is more consonant with the divine will than any other.

In the second place, the danger of seeking to impose a single political vision on others far outweighs any good that is likely to come of it. As Isaiah Berlin argued so tellingly in his famous lecture, 'Two Concepts of Liberty' (1958), the belief that a single pattern of social living is the goal of all people whether they know it or not, and that those who can grasp it have a duty to see it established for the benefit of all, is one that can lead to the worst forms of authoritarian government and the extinction of individual freedom. Christians may well believe (for example) that their faith implies a radical redistribution of private property in order to remove the scandal of a workless and land-less 'underclass' within a wealthy society; but as soon as they begin to try to gain adherents for a political programme that would put this into effect they are embarking on a course that could well lead to the coercion of those who would be disadvantaged by it. No liberal political system could survive the success of such an attempt.

In the third place, the primary model for a Christian vision of society is 'eschatological', that is to say, it is a form of society which does not yet exist and cannot exist until its time has come in the providence of God. This does not mean that it is a utopia, which means literally 'no place at all'. It is not a state of affairs that could never come about; but it requires the active intervention of God to bring it about. In the mean time, since the Kingdom has not yet come, every political system is bound to fall far short of the promised consummation, even if (as Christians believe) there may be signs of its dawning in certain historical situations. To seek to bring about the Kingdom by political action here and now is 'to take the kingdom by force' and pre-empt the timetable God has set for its realization. Which is not to say, of course, that there should not be an earnest pursuit of justice as a necessary precondition for the advent of any such 'Kingdom'; this pursuit is precisely one which may be shared with the great majority of fellow citizens. But when a pattern of social living allegedly inferred from Scripture and thereby invested with high authority is proclaimed as God's will for human beings and promoted by political (or even violent) action, then realities known only to faith and promised only in God's providential time are being misappropriated as a charter for immediate action, in defiance of those very liberal principles on which a 'Christian' society rightly prides itself.

The church as a model?

The church, however, is itself a society; and within that society Christians are free to organize themselves in whatever way they believe is consonant with the principles of authority revealed in their Scriptures. Their association with one another for the purposes of proclaiming and spreading their faith, of mutual care and assistance, and of stewardship of buildings and resources, gives to the church a political character and places it in need of leadership, government and procedures for the settlement of disputes. Can it therefore serve as a model for secular political institutions?

Certainly there is material in the Christian Scriptures which appears to reveal the type of government which should be adopted. Individual congregations were from very early times served by ordained ministers – bishops, priests and deacons – and maintained close contact with one another through a central authority and through meetings of their senior representatives. They were to have a systematic care for their poorer members and a ministry of healing among themselves. And they were to settle disputes in their own courts in preference to having recourse to those of the secular government. These precedents have been held to provide a skeleton framework for the church's institutional life. But even so they fall far short of a 'constitution'. For this, right from the start, the church has had to draw on the experience of existing forms of government, which it has adapted to its own use with varying success. In one (the dominant) tradition authority has been hierarchical, the three orders of ministry established in the early church being regarded as normative for any authentic church organization (despite the fact that the third order, of 'deacons', has never found a lasting role for itself). In another, mainly post-Reformation, tradition the principle of shared authority and collective responsibility which seems implicit in the gospel has made the establishment of a 'presbyterian' form of government take priority over the scriptural references to the early existence of bishops or other ordained office holders. In addition, there is a haunting saying of Jesus with profound organizational implications – 'the least shall be greatest among you' – a principle which it seems never to have been possible to put into institutional practice (except to a very limited degree within monastic communities). Accordingly the pattern of the church's political organization has varied greatly at different times and places, and has been no less subject to corruption and the abuse of power than any other. Indeed the only respect in which it can be said to be superior to purely secular forms of government is that it is acknowledged to be *semper reformanda*, always subject to the gospel which it is charged to proclaim and from which human sinfulness will always cause it to decline. There is certainly no single model of church government which can be confidently held up as a model for the world to emulate.

Indeed the objection to using church structures as a model for political institutions is more serious than this. The world in which most of us live is now totally committed to democracy.

Admittedly this is often no more than a slogan. 'One person one vote' by no means guarantees a system we would be prepared to call 'democratic'. Other rules and conventions need to be in place: governments must seek re-election every few years; there must be no discrimination of gender, race or class among those seeking office; the judiciary must work independently of the executive; there must be freedom of speech and information. But on all such tests the churches are liable to fail. Their ministers may be in post for life (or at least until retirement); some ministerial offices may be closed to women; church judgments affecting individuals may be pronounced by the same persons as are responsible for government and administration; there may be censorship of open discussion and control of teaching institutions. The churches – and the same applies to the structures of most other religious communities – are far from democratic. Yet their members find in their faith powerful reasons to support and promote democratic government: the dignity of each human being as a child of God, the responsibility committed to every bearer of political power for the welfare of others, the requirement that society should care for its weakest and most vulnerable members – these principles are shared by all the great religions and arguably find their most valid political expression in some form of democracy. Christians, like members of other faiths and of none, should certainly be alert to the failings of any political system and be ready to criticize it openly; but their record in managing their own affairs, their undemocratic procedures and the uncertainties that surround the interpretation of the scriptural warrants for their own constitutions make it impossible for them to propose their own authority structures as a model for any society outside their own membership.

But if it is illegitimate, and even possibly dangerous, for Christians to commend a form of government that should be adopted by the political leaders of the nation in which they live, this is not to say that they may not find in their faith valid reasons to criticize the actual conduct of public affairs and advance proposals for political reform. This is in fact what has been done by Christian political thinkers down the centuries:

throughout the Middle Ages it was taken for granted that the church, as guardian of the laws of God which held sway over all human institutions, would be watchful over the conduct of rulers in meeting the claims of righteous government; and in more recent times Christians have made their contribution to the development of 'political economy' and to the search for alternatives to the *laissez-faire* economic doctrines which prevailed until the mid-nineteenth century. The Christian Socialists, in particular, alerted the Anglican and Protestant churches to the need to bring Christian principles to bear on the social injustices that were the legacy of the industrial revolution; the papal teaching that began with *Rerum Novarum* in 1891 aligned the Roman Catholic Church decisively with resistance to the unregulated exploitation of labour and initiated a century of sustained 'social teaching'; and in recent years liberation theology has mounted an attack on the oppressive regimes of Latin America which has had an influence far outside that continent. It would be ungrateful to suggest that this Christian social thinking has not been a valuable contribution to public awareness and political debate.

Motivation and doctrine

Yet it is necessary to distinguish. Christians may find in their faith a strong motivation for entering the political struggle and working for a better society; they may also believe that Christianity provides guidelines for their political action. So far as motivation is concerned, there is no doubt that Christian faith, spirituality and personal experience may have a profound influence on a person's sensitivity to social and economic wrongs. The Christian Socialists of the nineteenth century were motivated by an 'incarnational' theology. In reaction to the current tendency to separate religion from public affairs and to confine Christian teaching to personal and 'spiritual' matters, they protested that Jesus Christ was incarnate *in* the full realities of everyday life and that any true discipleship must reflect his concern for the poorest and most disadvantaged of our fellow men and women. This led them to dedicate themselves to the well-being of the poor and to work on practical schemes for social reform. Similarly, in the second half of the twentieth century, close personal contact with the very poor in Latin America and recognition that the poorest *campesinos* could see meanings in biblical texts which had for centuries escaped the notice of more sophisticated Christians led priests and theologians to revise their Christian priorities and dedicate themselves to the 'liberation' of the oppressed. In 1985, as we saw, the team of clergy and lay experts which compiled *Faith in the City* was so scandalized by the alienation from the mainstream of national life of a whole swathe of the population of England, and found in the social and economic deprivation of urban areas such a contradiction of their Christian values, that they issued a call to both church and nation for an end to this 'grave and fundamental injustice'. In all these cases the Christian faith provided powerful motivation. The plight of the poor, their disempowerment and their deprivation of the most elementary rights and opportunities, aroused more than sympathy: it seemed such an offence to their Christian perception of justice and human dignity that they could do no other than press for political remedies.

But to say that their Christian faith alerted them to the problem and roused them to action is not to say that it also provided them with answers. It did not even necessarily enable them to ask the right questions. When F. D. Maurice enunciated his famous principle that society cannot be governed by competition but must give place to cooperation, he had certainly identified one of the driving forces of capitalism but he failed to recognize that competition has good attributes as well as bad: within a family it would be absurd to suggest that two gifted siblings should not develop their skills by competing with each other; what matters is that the winner should not maltreat or despise the loser and that the loser should not lose self-respect. It is the same in business: competition is reasonably held to be vital for promoting the quality of production; criticism is justified only when there is unfair advantage or where the work of the loser is undervalued. Similarly the profit motive, and an economic climate which appears to put self-interest above service to others, is easy to criticize from a Christian standpoint; but such criticism is out of place where profits are ploughed back into the business and the operatives and directors are not rewarded on an unreasonable scale. The simple application of 'Christian virtues' (such as thrift or generosity), which are normally defined in terms of personal behaviour, to the realities of economic life is liable to lead to serious misapprehensions and ensure that the leaders of industry and commerce pay little attention to what the churches are saying. It has been part of the life work of the social theologian Ronald Preston to demonstrate that the weakness of much Christian comment on social affairs in the past has been, not its theology, but its imperfect grasp of economics.

Given, however, that Christian thinkers, at least since the middle of the nineteenth century, have correctly drawn attention to some of the evil effects of the dramatic economic and social processes which have been at work in the developed world up to our own time, we can ask by what criteria they judged these developments to be immoral and in conflict with their religious principles. To which the answer is that, for the most part, these criteria, however much they may have been the product of Christian moral attitudes in the past, are not distinctively Christian at all. Justice, freedom, human dignity, a caring society – these values occur again and again as the standard against which Christian theologians and church leaders measure the policies of governments and the quality of civil administrations. In doing so, of course, they find themselves supported by a wider swathe of public opinion than that of their own co-religionists, and are on correspondingly stronger ground than they would be if they were following a specifically 'Christian' line. (The official Vatican doctrine relating to contraception, which has lost the support of a large number of Roman Catholics as well as having little attraction for non-Catholics, is a good example of the danger of venturing into public affairs on the basis of a purely religious judgment which, though beginning

as a matter of personal discipline for the faithful, has implications – e.g. for world population control – for society as a
whole.) The example of William Temple, deservedly regarded
as one of the outstanding social theologians of the twentieth
century and one who gave definitive expression to the Christian
socialist tradition, is particularly instructive in this respect. His
Christianity and Social Order (1942) concluded with these
objectives for society: every child should find itself a member of
a family decently housed and should have the opportunity to be
educated up to adulthood; every citizen should have an income
adequate to maintain home and family and have two days of rest
a week and holidays with pay; all should enjoy freedom of
speech and of worship. Evidently these objectives are not laid
down in Scripture, nor could they easily be inferred from it.
Indeed Temple made no secret of the fact that his inspiration
was what he called 'the Natural Order or Natural Law'. In other
words, he was applying to society, not specifically Christian
insights at all, but principles which could be derived from a
widely shared ethical framework, dignified by the name 'Natural
Law'. In the words of the church historian Alan Wilkinson,
(*Christian Socialism*, 1998, p. 125) 'he articulated and did much
to consolidate the social consensus'. What he did *not* do – and he
would have forfeited much of his influence had he done so – was
to project on to the real world of political and economic
processes a set of theoretical principles that could have been subscribed to only by those who accepted the authority of Christian
Scripture and tradition.

Are there then no specific insights derived from social or
political theology which may legitimately be introduced into
public debate? Is there no direction in which Christians may
legitimately seek to move society as a result of their own religious convictions? Can religions do no more – important though
this may be – than provide a particular motivation for engaging
in the pursuit of those ideals and values which are generally
shared by the citizens of any civilized society? The answer to this
question may not be so bleakly negative as would at first appear.
We have already looked at certain protests and proposals which

have emerged from Christian and other religious thinking and
which give at least some substance to the claim that religions in
general, and Christianity in particular, have an important part
to play in 'civil society'. And there are others we must take into
account before we close. But first we must take note of some
subtle influences which may be exerted in the reverse direction,
and which provide an additional reason for caution in bringing
'theological' language into the sphere of public affairs.

10

Dangers of the bandwagon

We have been looking at a number of instances in which 'theology' has allegedly been enlisted to engage with matters of current concern. Before trying to establish a more reliable base for official church comment we should be aware that there may also be a movement in the opposite direction, current secular assumptions exercising an influence (often not realized till long afterwards) on theological thinking, even to the extent of creating a new 'theology' that is held to be normative for church policy and action, but may be seen subsequently merely to have led the church into conformity with a reigning ideology.

The most obvious example of this in recent times is the capture of the German Protestant churches by Hitler: the already somewhat humanist understanding of the faith held by many German theologians and church leaders in the early years of the twentieth century was easily harnessed to a worship of the Führer alongside Christ. It required a theologian as percipient and eloquent as Karl Barth to expose the extent of doctrinal corruption involved and to inspire the creation of what became the *Bekennende Kirche* of the resistance. Similarly, as is equally well known, the Dutch Reformed Church in South Africa was persuaded to support apartheid on allegedly theological grounds (involving a highly selective reading of the Old Testament) – a position which the authorities of that church officially repented of after the end of apartheid. But these theological developments took place under exceptionally powerful political pressure, and could be regarded as little more than theoretical justification for practical attitudes which church members felt personally forced to adopt. More significant for our purpose are those shifts in theological emphasis and those allegedly new theological perceptions which are the result of more or less unconscious assimilation to the unquestioned assumptions of the time.

The ecological bandwagon

We have already seen one notable example of this tendency in the case of 'the theology of work', where a growing realization of the social evil of unemployment created the assumption that 'work' is essentially good and set theologians on a quest to provide support for this assumption in Scripture. Another, more far-reaching, example is the exploitation of one particular text in the interests of science and technology. The great scientific innovators of the sixteenth and seventeenth centuries were for the most part profoundly religious men. They were encouraged to find in Genesis 1.28 ('fill the earth and subdue it, have dominion over the fish of the sea, the birds of the air and every living thing . . . ') divine authorization for pursuing a branch of knowledge which would lead to ever greater 'dominion' over natural forces and resources. In the nineteenth century scientists were still talking freely of 'wresting the last secrets from nature' or 'subduing the earth to our use', an enterprise fully endorsed, so they believed, by revealed religion. It was only when it began to become apparent that such a programme, pursued without restraint, posed a serious threat to the environment and ultimately to human well-being that theologians were persuaded to take another look at the Genesis text. They obligingly came up with a new interpretation of the words. 'Subdue' and 'dominion' were, they said, not appropriate translations: the text implied, not human domination, but cooperation with God in his creative activity and stewardship of the earth's resources. Biblical scholars may well protest that this is reading a lot into it; to which it will be replied that the words should always have been read in the context of human responsibility for the created order under God and that an unfettered 'dominion' could never have been intended. But what the episode shows is the ease with which biblical texts may be pressed into service to support any generally accepted assumption: the modern environmentalist has as little right cheerfully to assume biblical support for sustainable policies as the seventeenth-century Fellow of the Royal Society had to assume that he was promoting God's purposes by his experiments. The real agenda was being set by quite other considerations.

A similar and more subtle instance can be seen in the history of interpretation of the statement of St Paul in Romans (8.19–22) that the whole of creation was subjected to frustration, is 'groaning and travailing' until now and looks forward to its 'liberation'. When Paul wrote he was reflecting the belief of his culture that the present world order is imperfect and will give way at some future and perhaps imminent date to one that conforms to God's will and moreover that humans bear some responsibility for the present condition of the created order. This was well understood by his early commentators. But throughout the Middle Ages and indeed long after, when the world was thought of as an unchanging arena in which human beings must prepare themselves for the much more important life to come, these words became virtually unintelligible and were subjected to astonishing gymnastics of interpretation. Now, however, when responsibility for the continuance of a habitable world has once again been seen to rest with our own choices, St Paul's words have sprung back to life. There could be no better example of the way in which prior assumptions may influence our understanding and use of a scriptural text.

Poverty and riches

By way of introduction to an instance of the same tendency which comes much closer to the concerns of this book, let us refer again to the interpretation of another well-known biblical text, this time from the New Testament, which has been deeply influenced by the circumstances of its interpreters. The saying of Jesus that it is 'easier for a camel to pass through the eye of a needle than for a rich man to enter the kingdom of God' (Mark 10.25) very naturally aroused the astonishment of the disciples (given the prevailing assumption that wealth, properly acquired, is a sign of God's blessing) and caused them to ask, 'Then who can be saved?' Jesus' reply appears to concede that there may be exceptions: 'With men this is impossible but with God all things are possible'. But subsequent interpreters, the great majority of whom have been persons of adequate if not ample means, have seized on these last words as evidence of the gracious generosity of God. Countless Christians have been at least relatively wealthy; but God, who can do the 'impossible', will surely have made an exception for each and every one of them and admitted to the Kingdom all suitably well-intentioned and devout people, whatever their material circumstances. The saying, that is to say, is not really about personal wealth at all; it is about the measureless grace of God. Or so it has seemed to generations of comfortably off readers. It took a liberation theologian, writing out of the experience of constant intimacy with the very poor, to suggest that Jesus may have meant what he appears to have said. God may of course make exceptions – but real exceptions remain exceptional! In the normal way those who are wealthy simply are not candidates for the Kingdom, certainly not if their wealth (as is the case of most of us in the northern hemisphere) is gained at the expense of the great majority of peoples in the rest of the world whose poverty is near to starvation level and shows no sign of being lessened despite the increasing riches of the First World.

But has not liberation theology itself been influenced by a set of secular assumptions, namely those of Marxism? As we have seen, this has been the charge most eagerly taken up by its enemies. The fact that this theology has identified sin in 'structures' as well as individuals, has regarded the empowerment of the poorest classes as its first priority, has secured its most active support through 'base communities' that bear a resemblance to communist cells, and has at times used Marxist methods of economic and historical analysis, has made it easy for the opponents of all such popular movements to identify its proponents as 'communists' and to persecute those parts of the church which, on these grounds, can be represented as a threat to the established order. The famous saying of Dom Helder Camara, bishop of a desperately poor diocese in the north-east of Brazil, 'When I try to help the poor they call me a saint, when I ask why they are so poor they call me a communist', well illustrates the superficiality of the charge; as does Oscar Romero's reply to the same accusation, 'What do you think? Is this communism? This struggle of the *campesinos* to survive, to stay on those lands, to have a place to work . . . is it communism?' That the church should have so clearly identified itself with the very poor by no means justifies a charge of Marxist policies and intentions. Yet there is no doubt that some of the presuppositions which these theologians brought to their formulation of 'liberation' as a priority for Christian prayer and action were Marxist in origin and have continued to influence their 'theology' and even their biblical exegesis. A startling example occurs in an essay by Jon Sobrino ('The Crucified Peoples', *Concilium* 1990/6, pp. 120–129), in which he takes the famous Suffering Servant passage in Isaiah 53, and enumerates his attributes – a man of sorrows, accustomed to suffering, despised by men, submissive, not opening his mouth and so forth. Each of these attributes fits the suffering people of El Salvador. But this Suffering Servant prefigured Christ. The poor people of El Salvador are therefore themselves, like the Servant, a 'crucified people' in which Christ is present today and with whom the church should therefore be totally identified – with the inevitable implication that those who are fortunate enough to be less poor can *not* be so identified with the suffering of Christ: in much of these theologians' preaching there is little salvation offered to the rich unless they somehow identify and struggle with the poor. This is a clear case of finding support in a biblical text for a position evidently reached on other grounds. These grounds were simply that the situation was a 'grave and fundamental injustice' and that Christians who come into close contact with the very poor cannot but throw themselves into the struggle for their 'liberation'.

A similar example nearer home (though at the other end of the political spectrum) was the enlistment a few years ago of some prominent theologians in 'dialogue' with industry and commerce. It was said that the churches, by showing a lack of interest or even implicit disapproval towards economic productivity, were actually discouraging people from going into business: could they not see that a prosperous industrial and financial sector was vital not just for the prosperity of the country but in order to make resources available for the charitable work which the churches themselves have so much at heart? The principle assumed to be held in common on both sides of the dialogue was that 'the creation of wealth' is necessary and desirable; how it is created, and how distributed once created, are important but secondary questions, to be settled by an exercise of fine tuning between commercial interests and ethical (or 'Christian') considerations.

The theologians responded by willingly participating in debate. They accepted the premise that the creation of wealth is a desirable objective, for which they found support, once more, in Genesis 1.28: it was a natural inference from 'be fruitful and multiply, fill the earth and subdue it'. They stressed, naturally, that distribution is important: if more wealth is created it must not be for the benefit of only a few; and they raised concerns about the quality of products, conditions of work and protection of the environment. By so doing they doubtless exercised some wholesome influence on the world of business, though many in that world would justifiably protest that they already share these concerns and do not need to be reminded of them by church people. But what, it seems, the theologians failed to do was to question the basic premise of the discussions. Given that it is now established beyond contradiction that the increasing wealth of the developed world has *not* made the rest less poor, that neither natural resources nor the environment could possibly sustain the extension of the First World's standard of living to the entire global population and that a high degree of injustice is dangerously endemic in the pursuit of ever increasing production, serious questions needed to be asked about 'creation of wealth' as an agreed objective; but the 'theology of wealth creation' (like the 'theology of work') was already established as a legitimate programme of study and dialogue and seemed to preclude going back to ask the fundamental questions. The presuppositions of a secular discipline had fatally permeated theological discourse.

Church organization

The same tendency can be seen even when the church is reflecting on itself and contemplating reform of its structures. The Church of England has recently been through an ambitious exercise of reorganization (following upon the 'Turnbull Report', *Working as One Body*, 1996), resulting in the creation for the first time of a central executive body called the Archbishops' Council. Clearly modelled on a business or financial board of directors, this body is charged with 'strategic thinking and planning', in the expectation that the church at its lower levels (that is, the dioceses and parishes) will faithfully carry out its 'policies' and respond to its 'direction' and 'articulated vision'. Not only is the language transparently borrowed from the managerial culture of modern business; the whole concept is a startling break with a tradition of church life that goes right back to the New Testament, according to which initiatives and inspiration arise from small groups or associations within the church and are then brought into some degree of coordination or subjected to some control and revision by higher authorities. Passing down 'strategy' from above is altogether foreign to the character of the church throughout most of its history. What theological justification is offered for such a radical change?

The Turnbull Report was not short on theology; but it used some questionable concepts. The church, it argued, is endowed with 'gracious gifts' (not a scriptural phrase) for the proper management of its mission and service; and among these is 'leadership' (which is now to be vested in a central council). But 'leadership' is barely a New Testament word. Though a common word in secular Greek, it occurs only three times (always in Hebrews 13). Nor is the work of apostles or other ministers ever described by images taken from activities where 'leadership' naturally belongs – military operations, political initiatives or expeditions of exploration. Instead, New Testament writers use the word 'ministry', which has quite different connotations, placing service at the heart of any authority exercised in the church. The tasks of these 'ministers' are not 'dictating policy' or 'strategic planning', but rather discerning needs and opportunities for Christian mission and service, disciplining where necessary, encouraging and consoling. 'Leadership' may of course be exercised by, say, a bishop or a parish priest when there is some crisis or in pursuit of some agreed goal. But the understanding even of this has changed in recent years. Until about a generation ago the accepted style of leadership for a parish priest was directive, patriarchal and centripetal. Then came 'lay leadership', relieving the priest of some of his responsibilities. More recently a non-directive, enabling and collaborative style has become standard in clergy training. Meanwhile, as we have seen, in community work a new model is emerging, that of the 'social entrepreneur'. But none of this is noticed in the Turnbull Report. It is simply assumed that 'leadership' is required by the church, which is assured of receiving it by the fact that it is one of God's 'gracious gifts'.

Not that there is anything new about importing non-biblical concepts into an account of the church's organization. It is true that there is in most churches one historic strand of organizational continuity. That 'since the apostles' time there have been three orders of ministry', though by no means 'evident unto all men diligently reading Holy Scripture' (as the preface to the Ordinal in the BCP rashly claims), is an ancient tradition faithfully preserved in the Anglican Church. But even if this gives one a kind of grammar with which to define the relationship of these ministers with one another and with the church as a whole, it does not say much about their function. Whatever the theological definition of a bishop, in practice he may have been the senior pastor of a small town community, the bishop of a diocese covering nearly half of England, a prelate close to the springs of political power, a monk, or an ecclesiastical dignitary with no see or jurisdiction at all. A presbyter may have been a low profile elder in a congregation or the embodiment of a high sacerdotal ideal. A deacon has seldom had any distinct role at all, serving mainly to complete the grammatical necessity of a triadic ministry and preserving in the title a precious resonance of the emphasis placed by Jesus on service. The style of leadership and the roles these ministers have adopted have always been influenced less by theological reasoning than by secular and functional priorities.

This makes it all the more important to scrutinize these priorities, especially when they are dressed up in theological language. It is perfectly clear in this case that the presuppositions behind the reforms derived from a managerial culture in which phrases such as 'strategic planning', 'articulated vision', are at home and in which it is (or rather was, because this culture is changing fast, leaving the church, as usual, some way behind) taken for granted that 'policy' is decided at top level by an executive board, whose decisions are then carried out lower down in the organization. How inappropriate this is to the Church of England becomes obvious the moment one thinks of some of the great reforming movements and church initiatives of the past: the Evangelical Revival, the Oxford Movement, the nineteenth-century missions in other continents and in the new industrial cities, the ecumenical movement – none of these was devised in a central board room. But once the managerial model takes hold, it begins to influence the whole style of the church's administration, as is beginning to be seen in its larger institutions such as cathedrals or colleges, where the pastoral priorities of the past are giving place to the pursuit of efficiency and 'productivity'. Before so readily adopting the nostrums of a business culture, theologians and church leaders might have reflected that it is a culture which has for the most part left male domination and racial prejudice unaffected, has signally failed to redress an ever growing gap between the richest and the poorest, and has devalued individuals (making them dispensable in the name of efficiency) in a way little better than the capitalist treatment of the labour force in the nineteenth century against which the social teaching of the popes so rightly protested.

Individualism

But arguably the most pervasive, and perhaps the most perni-
cious, influence on theology is the individualism which has been
characteristic of the Western intellectual world ever since the
Enlightenment. We have already seen how this has influenced
thinking on human rights and the theology with which the
churches have tried to undergird them. And indeed its influence
can be traced in so many aspects of life and thought today that it
would be surprising if religion had been impervious to it. The
history of this individualism can plausibly be traced right back
to the Pre-Socratic philosophers who proposed that reality must
consist of tiny, unchanging particles mysteriously brought into
relation with one another in such a way as to make up the
universe which we perceive with our senses. Developed by
Epicurus as a philosophy with profound moral and spiritual
implications (liberating human beings from all superstitious
fears and from vain aspirations to interfere with the immutable
processes of nature), and clothed by Lucretius in passionate and
imaginative poetry, this way of visualizing reality inspired
Renaissance thinking and stimulated astonishing advances of
science. Physical phenomena were analysed into ever smaller
discrete units until modern physics came by its own route to find
'atoms' at the basis of all matter. By a similar process the
Cartesian separation of mind and body envisaged each as an
entity entirely separate from the other, giving rise to a dualism
that it took centuries to overcome. Later on, sociology accepted
without question an analysis of society according to which
human beings are basically Robinson Crusoes who just happen
to be living at close quarters with one another and whose
behaviour can be accounted for as the aggregate of innumerable
individual choices; just as political philosophy, as we have seen,
imagined men and women to have existed originally as totally
autonomous beings, only some mythical compact having
enabled them to work out the necessary compromises by which
they could live together without violence. It is not surprising that
theology took a similar route and sought to infer rights, duties,

obligations and goals from the 'nature' of human beings as discrete, individual persons created in the image of God.

But in recent years this pervasive atomism has begun to give way to a more 'social' model. Science itself has changed dramatically from the study of static, changeless elements to a recognition that reality is better defined as energy (not unlike the 'fire' of Heraclitus), that nothing is unchanging and that the smallest particles can be understood only in relation to one another. Similarly with the social sciences: 'social psychology', studying the behaviour not of individuals but of groups and communities, has taken its place beside the individualistic schools of Freud and Jung. Even economics has begun to recognize that economic behaviour is not accounted for simply by the choices of individuals but by preferences which owe much to the instincts of people in groups and communities. The popularity of the word 'holistic' itself reveals a reaction in many people's minds against an atomistic approach; and the sense that somehow, despite immense advances in technical understanding and power, something precious has been lost called 'community', has set in train a vigorous quest for new forms of old associations and brought about some of the remarkable ventures in 'community' which we described in Chapter 6.

So far, however, there is little sign of a comparable development in the official theology of the churches. Individual theologians have certainly addressed the question, drawing attention to the essentially social character of human beings in the Bible (finding their identity in tribe and nation in the Old Testament, in a new community, the Body of Christ, in the New), and sometimes arguing (in a way we have seen to be precarious) from the 'social' (but in fact only threefold) nature of the Trinity to the essentially social nature of human beings; and an occasional gesture towards this sociality is made in recent Roman Catholic social teaching (e.g. *Lumen Gentium*, §125) But for the most part church comment on social affairs continues to begin with Genesis 1 and with human beings created 'in the image of God', with an occasional reference to Genesis 2.18 ('It is not good that the man should be alone') to explain the necessity of social existence. The conclusions which can be inferred from this single premise are fatally limited. The status of the isolated individual is an altogether inadequate base for the social obligations and aspirations which belong to any satisfying form of life in fellowship with others.

It seems to be time, that is to say, for the churches to recognize that their understanding of human beings has been deeply conditioned by a particular era of thought and has been left behind by the main intellectual disciplines of today. Reality itself is no longer seen as an assembly of discrete individual particles but as an infinitely intricate network of interactive forces – a butterfly wing in Europe 'causing' a tempest in Japan. Human beings can no longer be usefully studied as discrete individuals: everything they do, or even think, is conditioned (even if not necessarily determined) by the circumstances in which they happen to be set and by their relationship with one another and with their environment. That we are made in the image of God is a precious truth of revelation; but it must now be held together with the equally important knowledge of our basically social nature which comes to us from many other sources and which was indeed taken for granted at an earlier period of the church's history.

It is taken for granted also in the Bible. The interpretation of the central themes of Paul's theology has suffered ever since the Reformation from what has been called 'the introspective conscience of the West'. 'Justification' has been assumed to be a matter for the individual, to be obtained by careful soul-searching to ensure that one was not relying on any sense of having fulfilled 'the Law' – a set of moral regulations imposed from outside oneself. But 'fulfilling the Law' would have made no sense to Paul as a project for an isolated individual: it meant the decision to belong to a community whose common life was governed by the observances it prescribed. The decision to be justified by Christ alone instead of by the Law was the decision to identify oneself, not with a community bound to legal observances, but with the new community created by the act of faith in Christ. So also with the Beatitudes: Jesus does not say, 'Blest is the poor person', but, 'Blest are the poor' – that whole confraternity of people whose relations with one another are determined by their poverty. And indeed the same goes for the central doctrines of Christianity. 'As in Adam all die, so in Christ shall all be made alive' (1 Cor. 15.22). The doctrine of the atonement itself depends on a corporate understanding of humanity: we 'all die' in Adam because of our solidarity with one another, we have the benefit of Christ's resurrection because of our solidarity with him through faith, which is also a new solidarity with one another. In the Bible no single, totally unrelated person is treated as the object of our redemption.

In short, Christians need to build on Aquinas's perception (which was derived from Aristotle as well as from the Bible) that society is not something from which people simply take what they have a right to but which gives to individuals what they could not have on their own. It is in this sense that he wrote that 'every law is ordered to the common good' (*Summa*, I IIae 90.2) – not to the good of the individual. Christians must free themselves from those individualistic premises which have governed so much of their thinking, praying, acting and even Bible reading over the last three hundred years. Only so can the churches hope to make a significant contribution to the solving of the great social issues which lie before humanity today.

11

Diversity and community

We have assumed up to this point that there is likely to be a 'Christian view', generally supportive of a wider moral consensus on matters of social and political concern. But even if there is often a *majority* Christian view, there is likely just as often to be a minority in profound disagreement. Does this invalidate any Christian contribution? And is the alleged 'theological' problem the real cause of the disagreement? One or two examples will help to clarify the question and may at the same time help us to see how a Christian contribution to these issues actually takes effect.

War and peace

The first example is provided by the responses Christians have made to the problem of war and violence. On the one hand there appear to be clear gospel teachings which prohibit any form of violence, which enjoin love of all, even of enemies, and which show non-resistance to evil to be the Christian way – the way followed by Jesus himself to its bitterest, but in the end triumphant, conclusion. A simple reading of these texts seems to give a clear message that any faithful Christian should be a pacifist. But on the other side stands the apparent obligation, laid on Christians as much as on any one else, to punish crime, to maintain civil order and to defend oneself and others against violent attack. How do Christians live with this tension, and how does it affect their readiness to engage in serious discussion of issues of peace and war?

The majority of Christians down the centuries have been more influenced by their sense of civic responsibility than by the radical demands of the gospel and consequently have been prepared to bear arms and engage in war. The necessary restraints under which they should do so have been worked out in the tradition of the Just War, which was first formulated by St Augustine and which itself rests on philosophical premises that are much older. This tradition is arguably still very much alive (it was frequently invoked on both sides of the controversy over the justification for the Gulf War in 1991). Indeed it offers as good an example as one could wish of Christians making their contribution to the public debate over an issue of national importance on the basis of a widely shared moral consensus – in this instance, that the military operations must be for 'a just cause', be 'proportionate' to the ends to be achieved, be undertaken only as a 'last resort' and so forth. Admittedly there are certain respects in which the Just War tradition may be regarded as out of date. The real and potential conflicts which challenge the West today are often not of the character which was envisaged when Just War thinking was formulated. Until recently, questions of war, peace and armed intervention were raised by the actions of one nation state against another. Today the most common form of violent action takes place not between states but within them; and the international community is much exercised over whether there is legal and moral justification for intervening. The principles that now have to be applied perhaps have less to do with the 'justice' criterion of the Just War tradition than with the perceived humanitarian necessity to prevent serious abuses of human rights and genocide. But the effect is the same: the moral standards being invoked in the public debate are those which are generally shared by the public. The distinctively Christian contribution is to lay particular emphasis upon the promotion of peace and justice and to put weight behind those who are seeking to prevent the issue being distorted by the national self-interest of any of the parties. Numerous church reports and public statements have exhorted governments along these lines.

Yet there have always been some, and in the last century and

a half they have been an articulate and often well organized
minority, who regard this approach as a betrayal of the principles of Christianity and have committed themselves to the
pacifist position. Their primary motive has always been what
they have understood to be an unequivocal demand of the
gospel; but there are also good common-sense arguments in
their favour – for example, that war never actually does any
good, that non-resistance has seldom been wholeheartedly tried
but that when it has (as in the case of Gandhi) it has shown itself
remarkably effective, that reconciliation after violent conflict is
often impossibly difficult and the hatred engendered is always
liable to break out afresh. It is arguments such as these, along
with an instinctive revulsion from bloodshed and destruction,
which persuade many who are not Christians to adopt the
pacifist position. But it is the sense that an absolute refusal to
resort to violence is the only valid response to the teaching and
example of Jesus which gives profound and even passionate
conviction to the Christian pacifist, whose witness (often heroic)
remains a challenge to the majority of church people who accept
the other view.

Yet one thing about which pacifists are for the most part
perfectly clear is that they can never hope or expect to persuade
an entire nation to follow their example. They recognize that
even if they were in the majority they would have no right to
deprive others who disagreed with them of protection against
violent criminals or invading armies. Their contribution, that is
to say, wins respect because it has good reasons to support it and
is adhered to at very considerable personal cost by those who
offer it. It continues to challenge others because it corresponds
to a deep human yearning – for a society which lives at peace
with itself and its neighbours without the use or threat of force.
When made by Christians, it has the added force of being a
persuasive (though not the only) interpretation of Christian
fundamentals. To many, the pacifist ideal will always seem
utopian – as indeed the ethic of Jesus may. For this reason it
cannot be advanced as a realistic programme of political action.
But the witness of a substantial minority of Christians who are

prepared to risk their security and even their lives rather than abandon it remains a precious element in the consciousness of the many who would willingly abjure the use of force if only they could be satisfied that they were not failing to fulfil their responsibilities as citizens of a nation which still needs protection from enemies without and within. As we shall see, this is a powerful analogy for the role which distinctively Christian thinking may play in public affairs in general.

It is a remarkable but seldom noticed fact of church history that the division between mainstream Christians who accept the need for armed force in certain circumstances and pacifist Christians who are prepared to die rather than take up weapons themselves – which on the face of it is a fundamental difference of doctrine in a matter of great practical importance – has never caused a major schism in the church. Apart from small groups such as the Quakers, the churches have been able to hold these two opposing stances within a single Christian family. Pacifists will of course be inclined to regard non-pacifist Christians as failing to face up to the rigour of the ethical demands made by Jesus: anyone who is prepared to use force against another human being for any purpose whatever appears to them to be evading the clear message of the gospel that violent action can never be the Christian way. Non-pacifists, for their part, while they may respect the pacifists' position and admire the courage with which it is held, will tend to think that they do not take sufficiently seriously the obligation of every Christian to pursue justice and maintain peace, an obligation which may well require the use of force when the innocent are attacked and when justice and peace are threatened. The truth is, of course, that this is a case where two major principles of the Christian life may be in conflict – the absolute prohibition of the use of force even in self-defence (which seems to follow from the commands to love one's enemies and not to retaliate against evil) and the responsibility of every individual for the safety and well-being of fellow citizens (which follows from the beatitude, 'Blessed are those who hunger and thirst to see right prevail', and from some of the apparent implications of 'loving one's neighbour as oneself'). This is a conflict that cannot be wished away, and it is inevitable that Christians should not all come down on the same side. The significant thing is that the two sides have come to respect each other, and there is no suggestion that one position is less 'Christian' than the other and ought to be excluded from the options open to an orthodox member of the church. Moreover this respect has now become a principle of national life in many countries (though it is alien to the Muslim tradition): for the last century or so conscientious objectors have had the right to refuse military service in times of war, a provision which in 1987 was recognized by a UN Commission as a Human Right and has been justly called one of the marks of a civilized society.

This example is significant, not least because it shows that Christians do not necessarily have to agree in order to make an impact on national life. Pacifists have done so because of their personal integrity in a cause which, though the majority find it impractical, nevertheless responds to a deep human yearning for a world in which swords are beaten into ploughshares; Christian 'Just War' theorists have had an influence because of the reasonableness of their objections to the excessive or indiscriminate use of force. Even this more pragmatic interpretation of Christian principles may result in opposition to public policy. Debate has raged for many years over the admissibility of 'nuclear deterrence': is it morally justifiable to threaten an adversary with the destruction of entire cities, even if it can be argued that it is precisely this threat which has up to now prevented war from breaking out between nuclear powers? The Just War principle of discrimination, backed up by the traditional catholic teaching that the innocent are to be protected at any cost, has created a powerful lobby, joined by many who are not Christians, in opposition to the British government's reliance on an independent nuclear deterrent. But again, there are reflective Christians who conscientiously believe that the deterrence policy is both justified and necessary. The fact that there is disagreement within the churches (as there is in the public at large) does not rob the Christian contribution of its value. Because the principles on which it is based are widely shared (even if they lead people to different conclusions) it at least has the effect of helping others to form a responsible and well-informed view.

Poverty and wealth

A similar case is presented by the so-called 'preferential option for the poor' which has been a principle of Vatican teaching for the last few decades. In reality there are once again two principles in conflict. On the one hand there is the tradition, inherited from Thomas Aquinas, of the sanctity of private property: an individual has an absolute right to the enjoyment of property which has been honestly acquired. No appeal to justice, no revolutionary movement has the right forcibly to deprive people of that which they legitimately own. On the other hand stands a virtually inexorable economic law (well known in the Old Testament and in classical Antiquity) that unless there is some regulation the rich will tend to get richer and the poor poorer. In Latin America, where this process has resulted in the pauperization of the great majority of the population, it has come to seem to many an absolute Christian duty to identify with the poor and work for some redistribution of their countries' wealth, even though this will mean the forcible reduction of the personal fortunes of some of the wealthy. To liberation theologians it seems at times inconceivable to give equal priority to the legitimate claims of the rich, and they have been inclined to say that it is impossible to be a Christian without showing a commitment to the empowerment of the very poor. This deeply felt identification with the impoverished masses has led the Roman Catholic Church to formulate its principle of a 'preferential option' for the poor. If this is understood in terms (which could be inferred from the Old Testament) of the necessity of preventing the legal and economic systems from being weighted in favour of the rich and powerful – as they will always tend to be if left to themselves – by a corresponding bias towards the interests of the poor, then all Christians may be ready to agree that this is a proper interpretation of the command to love one's neighbour, the neighbour most in need of this practical love being the poor. But if it means that the church is more concerned with the poor than the rich and is prepared to countenance the forcible redistribution of wealth, then there is a danger of the wealthy being actually unchurched instead of, as church members, having their conscience challenged by the realities of the poverty around them (to which, indeed, they may have wittingly or unwittingly contributed through a global economic system which has signally failed to prevent the wealthy nations from profiting from the poverty of the rest). As with pacifism, so with the 'preferential option for the poor': for all its resonances with the preaching of Jesus and the claims of the gospel, it must not be allowed to seem the only way in which Christians can witness to their faith. Those who find themselves far from poor may still be living according to Christian principles when they order their affairs with strict honesty and fairness and exercise generosity with their surplus.

The conflict between these principles is inevitable, and in some places puts great pressure on the solidarity between different social classes in the church. But (as in the case of pacifism) it has not yet caused a breakdown of communion, nor should it do so. Both sides may have good Christian reasons for the position they hold. But priorities may change. The conscience of Christians (as of others) is increasingly disturbed by the poverty of the majority of the world's population compared with the wealth of the majority, by the sheer weight of human suffering and deprivation which this involves, and by the tendency of the free global market (which has become almost an article of faith in developed countries) to increase the wealth of the few at the expense of the many. Resignation in the face of this apparent economic necessity is now suspect. May it not be just complicity for the sake of preserving one's own advantages? Accordingly the scales of management and distribution need to be tipped in favour of the poor if this evident injustice is to be addressed. Hence 'the preferential option for the poor', which represents a commitment, shared by the great majority of Christians in the West, to work towards the relief of acute poverty and a fairer distribution of the world's resources. This commitment, which has the conscientious support of a very large number of people (witness such popular events as Red Nose Day and Band-Aid) is a valid expression of Christian motivation in support of a widely perceived moral imperative.

Migrants and asylum seekers

There are other areas where Christian conviction and commitment may influence government policy, even if not unanimously supported by the churches. One such issue has recently grabbed the headlines. Only a decade ago a theologian offering Christian insights on the role of Britain in the European Union (David L. Edwards, *Christians in a New Europe*, 1990) was able to ignore completely one of the most significant factors, namely the movement of populations and the pressure of immigration from poorer and less-ordered countries. But now everyone is aware of the plight of the huge numbers of refugees and asylum seekers being forced to resort to ever more difficult means of illegal entry into European countries and the USA, many of them to escape intolerable conditions in their own countries (often involving torture, persecution and the threat of death). The dismantling of that scandalous obstacle to freedom of movement, the Berlin Wall, in 1989 has been followed by the erection of equally scandalous barriers against immigration, not simply legal and administrative but even physical – elaborate installations on the southern border of Mexico and the south coast of Spain to keep out unwanted immigrants from neighbouring impoverished continents. 'Fortress Europe' is a reality to which all European Union governments have acceded but which is an affront to the Christian conscience. Christianity is by no means alone among the world religions in having an explicit concern for the stranger, particularly the stranger in any kind of distress. Religious people are compelled by their faith to speak and act on their behalf. In major British cities the churches, along with mosques and synagogues, have been in the forefront of efforts to fill the gap left by recent changes in government provision for asylum seekers and to guarantee them not only the basic necessities of life but also some degree of dignity and self-respect.

There is, of course, powerful resistance to these efforts. Among the host population there is a natural instinct for self-preservation, which can easily be whipped up into a (largely unjustified) fear of the consequences of a 'flood' of immigrants claiming the host country's limited resources; and many people (including Christians) believe that there is reason to expect serious problems in race relations if there is a large influx of immigrants. But, once again, there is a powerful stock of natural sympathy and compassion to be tapped in any civilized society, and this can be enlisted by religious activists (particularly in the wake of well-publicized tragedies such as the fifty-eight victims of suffocation in a lorry full of Chinese refugees at Dover in 2000) to build up public support for a more humane immigration policy. Further reference to 'theological' reasons, such as the numerous biblical injunctions to respect the stranger in our midst, will not persuade many outside the churches (though it may strengthen the will of the faithful); but the Christian case can be reinforced by drawing attention to such practical considerations as the need for more skilled and youthful labour than the native population can provide, the anomaly of admitting unlimited foreign goods but not foreign workers, the virtual impossibility of administering fair adjudication on claims for asylum in such massive numbers and the undesirability of creating the conditions for criminal trafficking in refugees. All these factors may help to change the political climate in favour of a more generous policy. But the main appeal must always be to public sympathy for the fate of those who by any standard deserve our compassion and concern. The challenge to the churches and other religious bodies is to create a climate of opinion that politicians will be bound to respect. If they succeed, this will be another case where religious conviction and commitment will have had a real impact on public affairs, comparable in its way to the Christian impulse which in the end resulted in the abolition of the slave trade, despite the number of biblical texts that could be marshalled on the other side.

Community

Even though, as we have seen, official church theology has departed from the ancient priority given to the common good, relying instead on a doctrine of the human being treated as an isolated individual (a doctrine barely capable of sustaining the weight of social teaching erected upon it, particularly with regard to human rights), the churches, along with other religious communities, have maintained a strong interest in community, fellowship and creative cooperation, This has enabled them to articulate a widespread and instinctive anxiety about the importance claimed for unfettered competition in economic life and to strengthen the growing demand for the restoration of 'community' in social life. As we saw in Chapter 2, this was a prime concern of *Faith in the City* and has stimulated some lively thinking in the churches.

One example of this thinking is a report entitled *Church and Community Work* published by the Church of England Board for Social Responsibility in 1988. This report was the result of a year's work by a working party (which included others besides Anglicans) seeking to carry forward the thinking of *Faith in the City* and develop its practical application. It begins with a series of definitions and clarifications (much needed in this area) and then offers a section on 'Values and Theology' (§§16ff.). The 'values' consist of 'a vision of a cooperative society in which people live together peacefully and control the environment in which they live', a 'perspective on humanity that gives equal value to all people whatever their condition', a 'view of equality and justice', a commitment to power-sharing and an endorsement of genuine participation and collaborative styles of work. These principles are drawn, not from any distinctively Christian or theological principles, but from a general consensus on the goals to be aimed at, reinforced by experience of the results of good practice in community work. As such, they are likely to command widespread support.

The report then goes on (§17): 'It is also important to reflect on the connections between these values and the central themes in Scripture and the Christian tradition'. These themes include a

vision of the kingdom of God 'where all live in community and
koinonia', the search and struggle for justice and righteousness,
the preciousness and uniqueness of each person ('created in the
image of God but only able to be fully human when in relationship to others') and 'a memorable attentiveness to experience' (a
rather surprising theme justified by the statement that 'Jesus
found a way of relating to people that took their experience
seriously'). Notice the word 'connections'. It is not claimed that
these themes offer direct support to the values commended in
community work, nor are they developed or applied in any way
in the rest of the report – the only theological proposition which
is ventured later is the statement that 'enabling communities is
an essential part of Christian ministry' (§20). The most that is
claimed is that Christian people can find 'connections' in their
faith and be encouraged accordingly to commit themselves to
these values.

These paragraphs offer a good illustration of the answer, to
which our study has been leading, to the question, By what
authority can the churches speak about such matters? The
report is authoritative by virtue of the knowledge and experience of community work on which it draws. It is realistic in its
application to this work of values and objectives which are
generally regarded as desirable (though not every politician can
be expected to acknowledge 'the right of all people to have equal
chances of meeting human needs for income, housing, education, health and a safe environment', §16 c). It relies on a
widespread moral consensus. It then proceeds to 'connect ' this
consensus and these objectives with the Christian tradition,
indicating points at which the Bible can be shown to insist on
factors (such as *koinonia*, interrelatedness and the struggle for
social justice) which are at the heart of community work and
which should impel Christians to see their importance and
commit themselves to their promotion. This is summed up in the
sentences (§18), 'The Church, then, has a fundamental reason to
acknowledge the importance of community work. It also has
practical resources'. 'Acknowledging the importance' of values
and principles which are vital to our social flourishing and

encouraging Christians to proclaim them, to work for them and to make the most of their practical resources – this well summarizes the role which we have been led to see is that of the churches, as of other religious bodies, when they become involved (as they must) in social and economic affairs.

A common morality?

But is there really such a firm moral consensus in today's society that it is possible to say that we all know what is good and right, the only difference with Christians being that they are particularly strongly committed to it? In the 'plural' society in which we live, with its majority of professedly secular non-believers, and in a culture in which it is regarded as almost axiomatic that every individual has an absolute right to espouse the moral values of his or her preference, is it any longer possible, or even desirable, to speak of a shared morality? The post-modernist instinct is to assume a total relativism: all are entitled to their own beliefs, which include their own independent moral principles. Institutions which claim to represent a moral consensus, such as marriage, public decency, the churches, the monarchy, are declining in influence and deserve to do so since they infringe the basic right of all citizens to form their own judgments and fashion their own lifestyles. The challenge to government today is simply to ensure such order and tolerance as may enable the infinite diversity of individuals (more apparent than ever before through the mingling of cultures in most European states) to flourish. A common morality (on this view) is outdated and irrecoverable.

It is a view which certainly has influence. The shameless flouting of the decencies of intimacy, privacy and sexual restraint which is characteristic of large sections of the media owes much to a philosophical scepticism about the possibility of any shared standards. Yet at the same time there are aspects of our life which are governed by widely approved principles. The keeping of promises and the culture of trust in business, the general condemnation of corruption and pursuit of personal

gain in political life (witnessed to by continual investigations
into 'sleaze'), the almost universal support for human rights, the
huge public response to appeals for humanitarian aid, the
continued flourishing of charitable work of many kinds – it
would be a gross misdescription of modern society to say that
it has no shared moral standards. Indeed the existence of a
relatively stable political order itself is evidence of a public
consensus that political power requires legitimation and that the
rule of law is essential for a civilized society. Criminals, violent
anarchists, hooligans and extreme libertarians, whatever their
individual 'human rights' and 'civil liberties', must be restrained
for the sake of public order. A sense of fairness, justice and
decency continues to be the bedrock on which political action
and social cohesion is based. And behaviour which goes beyond
these basic principles – manifested in 'Christian' acts of generosity, self-sacrifice and compassion – continues to evoke widespread admiration. There will be differences of emphasis in
different religious and political groups – some may rate personal
freedom above cooperative achievement, others may place law
enforcement above personal liberty – but the overlap is substantial and enables government to continue on the basis of a broad
consensus.

   This, of course, to the religious mind, is what has been called
a 'thin' morality. As with the old debate on whether laws can
actually make people better, so with 'consensus morality': is this
enough to create and sustain a tolerable society? In the public at
large (assuming a mainly 'secular' society) the jury is probably
still out: people are aware that all is not well but are uncon-
vinced of the need for a 'thicker' morality to address their
problems. But religious people have little doubt. Sin is not the
same as law-breaking, law-abidingness is not the same as virtue,
concern for human rights does not of itself encourage social
responsibility. Stronger moral motivation is required – obedience to God's law, love of neighbour, willingness to forgo
personal gain for the good of others and so forth – if human
society is to flourish. This 'thickening' of morality may justly be
called 'theological'. It is on the basis of a specific understanding

of the Christian revelation that Christians – not always in agreement with one another but often in agreement with adherents of other religious faiths – may recommend a style of behaviour or programme of action which, if adopted, would have political implications for the rest of society. And here's the rub. The moment they go beyond what may be assumed to be a moral consensus, Christians must either confine themselves to addressing and exhorting their own fellow-believers or else be ready to subject their proposals to the test of political viability and acceptability. Hence, for example, the shy (and necessarily rare) appearance of concepts such as 'sacrifice' in the church documents we have been considering – the word occurs only once in the pope's summary of his church's social teaching in *Centesimus Annus* (1991). Christians can exhort one another to sacrifice their own interests for the good of others (though they will need to take care to establish that the sacrifice will make any difference to those whom they wish to help: for example, would a higher rate of income tax – which is often demanded by Christians in order to fund more adequate welfare provision – necessarily be used by the government in a way of which they would approve?); and they will find there is an answering echo in the willingness of many others to help those in need by forgoing their own advantage. But they cannot expect to be able to impose this 'theological' imperative on their fellow citzens in general. What they can do – and this is where the real contribution of religion to political realities lies – is make clear their own commitment to well-established ethical values and by their example help others to acknowledge and encourage those deeper springs of moral conviction which are fostered by stable family and community life and which are essential to the promotion of the common good.

12

Epilogue: 'Go and do likewise'

This conclusion of the parable of the Good Samaritan (Luke 10. 37) is the only instance in the Gospels of an explicit model being given for Christian behaviour. Jesus customarily challenges, rebukes, makes demands, calls to discipleship. What he does not do is tell stories with the moral, 'This is how you should behave'. Still less does he offer himself as an example to follow: those who are attracted by his teaching have to work out for themselves how they will respond. Some scholars have therefore doubted whether this injunction at the end of the parable goes back to Jesus at all: it could have been added by the evangelist, anxious to bring this troubling parable into line with the standard repertory of improving stories by which, then as now, people's moral character was formed. But for our purposes the point is un-important. What matters is that the model which has seemed throughout the centuries to provide the most powerful example of 'Christian' conduct is not some action of Jesus himself but is one drawn from behaviour which Jesus' hearers already recognized as morally compelling. The sting of the story was not some new standard of moral conduct or some 'theology' of Christian action; it was in the choice of a *Samaritan* to give the example, a race whom Jews disliked and despised. The thrust of the parable is then clear and characteristic of Jesus: if even a Samaritan behaves like this, how much more should you do yourselves? At the very least, go and do likewise!

Even if (as some have suggested) the parable owes more to Luke (the only evangelist who records it) than to Jesus, the style of teaching is certainly authentic. Jesus does not promulgate an entirely new moral code. Instead he draws attention to what is agreed to be most admirable in human behaviour and challenges his followers: why don't you do at least as well as that? His message, that is to say, assumes common ground with his hearers. They already know what is good and just. Their problem (like ours) is that they fail to do it, whether because of human weakness, or because they have interpreted the law of God in such a way that it provides a cloak for their evasions. By challenging moral complacency and tackling the roots of moral motivation he aims to raise the innate human qualities of love, generosity and compassion to new levels which would bring us closer to the divine nature and be worthy of the Kingdom.

Similarly with the early church. The moral injunctions in the New Testament epistles reflect the best moral practice which obtained in their world. It is very seldom that any distinctively 'Christian' teaching appears (Romans 12 is almost alone in sounding an echo of the Sermon on the Mount): the exhortations are cast in well-established modes of moral instruction, owing more to Stoic and Jewish traditions than to any new insights; indeed it was one of the favourite arguments of the Apologists of the second century that Christians did *not* behave differently from other people (and so could not be attacked as an outlandish or dangerous sect) – just better. Their moral code was basically the same as the best which existed in the culture in which they lived. And the same perception continued for many centuries to underlie Christian reflection on morality. The church based its ethical teaching, not on any radical principles derived from the gospels, but on a tradition of moral reasoning inherited from Stoicism (the reigning philosophy of the Roman Empire) which represented a general consensus on what was right and wrong in human conduct. This tradition, which became known as Natural Law, was regarded as the universal heritage of human kind, accessible to all whether or not they had received the benefit of the Christian revelation.

Of course it was true that Jesus had made demands which went well beyond these generally accepted moral standards; but these 'evangelical counsels' were, until the Middle Ages, regarded not as setting a new moral standard that all Christians must adhere to but as an ideal to which the most zealous might aspire. Subsequently they became the charter for a different lifestyle altogether, by which men and women, separating themselves from the world in religious communities, might conform themselves to Jesus' demands more closely than was possible for those engaged in secular pursuits. Since the Reformation further strategies have been employed to cope with these uncomfortable demands: they have been interiorized as dispositions rather than practical options (being theoretically ready to give one's life for others rather than actually doing so), or they have been regarded (especially by biblical critics) as being so conditioned by the time and place in which they were given that they are no longer applicable today. These 'strenuous commands' (as they have been called) continue to disturb the conscience of Christians and stimulate acts of great generosity and self-sacrifice; but the moral standards governing the lives of the great majority of church members have always been those which can be derived from a well-established philosophical tradition and are generally accepted in civilized societies. In most people's minds the 'Christian' way of doing things may be highly demanding but is not fundamentally different from that which most people would aspire to, nor is there a 'theology' of moral action totally different from the promptings of an ordinary person's conscience. Christians recognize that they are confronted by Jesus with an immensely demanding ethic; but the moral teaching with which they educate their children and seek to play their part in society has not attempted to incorporate his more radical injunctions and has mainly relied on a philosophical and prudential tradition which can be traced back well before his time and to which the great majority of his contemporaries subscribed.

But surely, it can be said, this is a faithless way of proceeding. Could not the church at least have a more Christ-like standard of ethical behaviour (willing self-sacrifice, generous giving, forgiveness of all personal offences) which would be expected of its members and could be held up to the world as an example for others to emulate? Could it not have a 'theology of social action' which would admittedly expect compliance only from

Christians but which might then inspire others to follow? This is the view of at least one influential moral theologian (the American Stanley Hauerwas), but it has to be said that experience (as well as more theoretical considerations) tells heavily against it. There has been no shortage of individual Christians whose lives have helped others to raise their moral standards, or of reformers in the churches who have tried to establish a more 'Christian' way of living among the faithful. But the difficulty of gaining general acceptance for any rules that would embody these standards and that would be accepted by all church members, let alone by society at large, has proved too great, and the danger of simply appearing to be 'holier than thou' and preaching a moral rectitude which those who preach it repeatedly fail to exemplify far outweighs any good that is likely to come of it. It has been a sound instinct of the churches through most of their history to proclaim a morality which is generally accepted by others as a desirable and practicable standard to aim at.

'Go and do likewise'

Jesus' most famous example of moral teaching consisted in drawing attention to the admirable behaviour unexpectedly shown by a despised foreigner and in challenging his hearers to do as much themselves. The churches, like other religious bodies, find deep resources in their Scriptures and traditional thinking to strengthen the resolve of their members to 'do likewise' and indeed to go far beyond the dictates of a commonly accepted morality. But, for all their 'theology', their appeal must ultimately be that of Jesus himself. This is the kind of action we all admire: let us do all we can to adopt it ourselves and persuade others to do the same.

But such advice, when offered in public statements and church reports, will have authority only on certain conditions. First, it must be tested against political realities no less than against the principles of any other relevant discipline. *Faith in the City* found a 'grave and fundamental injustice' in English national life. Its appeal was influential because this language resonates with the moral instincts of a large number of people and in the end compels political action. But the rectifying of injustice is a deeply political matter. The remedy involves some redistribution of material goods and political power. If this is not to be done by force (and Christians would normally be against this on principle) it requires the consent of those who will be deprived of some of their share of these things; and this consent will be gained, not by appealing to their religious or humanitarian feelings (though these may be a factor) but by strictly political considerations, such as the danger of inaction – social unrest or even revolution – and the gains for the cohesion of the community if the worst injustices are removed. The weakness of the report was not (as is so often alleged) its theology but its philosophy: it failed to place its judgments in the context of contemporary political realities. Failure to think through the political implications of morally persuasive proposals opens the churches to justified criticism from those who bear responsibility for their implementation in the real world of government and administration.

Secondly, any serious religious contribution to public affairs must also withstand the subtle pressures of contemporary language, fashions and ideologies. Catch phrases such as 'the creation of wealth', 'the superiority of the market', 'the rights of the individual' and 'the criterion of productivity' need to be carefully scrutinized before they are adopted into the theological agenda.

Thirdly, religious traditions must take account of the essentially social nature of human beings if they are to give adequate support to human rights and responsibilities. What is urgently required is the recovery of the concept of the human being in which social solidarity and obligation is a defining characteristic, not a subsequent adventitious attribute. Such a concept modern theology has so far been slow to supply. But without it there is no route in logic from the definition of humans as individual creatures made in the image of God to that common good which is the aspiration of us all.

Fourthly, it is essential to distinguish clearly between the 'theological' exhortations which may be offered to church members and the contribution that may be made to public debate on the basis of moral principles which are shared with the population at large. 'Political theology' is a subject of profound importance as an aid to understanding the way in which the Christian faith impinges on political issues; but when the appeal is to a wider public the argument needs to be supported by premises on which there is general agreement.

Above all, what is demanded of religious people of any faith, and indeed is arguably crucial to the survival of civilization itself, is that they should be constantly alert to infringements and erosions of the great moral principles which they share with an often silent majority of their fellow citizens and should be tireless in their determination, inspired by their faith, to rouse themselves and others to fight for a world in which these principles are universally respected.

Bibliography

Reports and statements

Roman Catholic

American Episcopal Conference, *War and Peace in the Nuclear Age*, London: CTS/SPCK 1983.
American Episcopal Conference, *Economic Justice for All: Catholic Social Teaching and the US Economy*, London: CTS 1986.
Bishops' Conference for England and Wales, *The Common Good*, London 1996.
Commission Sociale des Evêques de France, *Réhabiliter la Politique*, Paris: Centurion/Cerf/Fleurus-Mame 1999.
Vatican II, *Gaudium et Spes*, London: CTS 1965.
Vatican II, *Lumen Gentium*, London: CTS 1965.

Encyclicals

John XXIII, *Pacem in Terris*, London: CTS 1963.
John Paul II, *Laborem Exercens*, London: CTS 1981.
John Paul II, *Sollicitudo Rei Socialis*, London: CTS 1987.
John Paul II, *Centesimus Annus*, London: CTS 1991.
Leo XIII, *Rerum Novarum*, London: CTS 1891.
Paul VI, *Humanae Vitae*, London: CTS 1968.

Church of England

Archbishop's Commission on Urban Priority Areas, *Faith in the City: A Call for Action by Church and Nation*, London: Church House Publishing 1985.
The Church and the Bomb: Nuclear Weapons and the Christian Conscience, London: Hodder & Stoughton and CIO 1982.
General Synod, Board for Social Responsibility, *Perspectives on Economics*, London: CIO Publishing 1984.

Something to Celebrate: Valuing Families in Church and Society, London: Church House Publishing 1995.

A Time to Heal: A Contribution towards the Ministry of Healing, London: Church House Publishing 2000.

Working as One Body (the 'Turnbull Report'), London: CIO 1996.

Other

Council of Churches for Britain and Ireland, *Unemployment and the Future of Work: an Enquiry for the Churches*, London: CCBI 1997.

1 By what authority?

Bauckham, Richard, *The Bible in Politics: How to Read the Bible Politically*, London: SPCK 1989.

Belo, F., *A Materialist Reading of the Gospel of Mark*, Maryknoll: Orbis 1977.

Church of Scotland, *Report of Special Commission on the Ethics of Investment and Banking*, ?Edinburgh 1988.

Ellis, Marc, *Toward a Jewish Theology of Liberation*, London: SCM Press 1987.

General Synod Board for Social Responsibility, *Cybernauts Awake! Ethical and Spiritual Implications of Computers, Information Technology and the Internet*, London: Church House Publishing 1999.

Gutiérrez, Gustavo, *A Theology of Liberation*, London: SCM Press 1974.

Harvey, A. E. (ed.), *Theology in the City*, London: SPCK 1989.

Meeks, Wayne A., *The Origins of Christian Morality*, Yale: Yale University Press 1993.

Miranda, José P., *Marx and the Bible*, London: SCM Press 1977.

Preston, Ronald H., *Religion and the Ambiguities of Capitalism*, London: SCM Press 1991.

Rowland, Christopher, and Corner, Mark, *Liberating Exegesis*, London: SPCK 1990.

2 Faith in the City *and* The Common Good

Atherton, John, *Faith in the Nation*, London: SPCK 1988.

Church of England Board for Social Responsibility, *Prisons, a Study in Vulnerability*, London: Church House Publishing 1999.

Schreiter, Robert J., *Constructing Local Theologies*, London: SCM Press 1985.

Sheppard, David, *Bias to the Poor*, London: Hodder & Stoughton 1983.

Walker, Nigel, *Why Punish?* Oxford: Oxford University Press 1991.

3 *'The Theology of Work'*

International Labour Office, *World Employment*, 1996/7.

Oldham, J. H., *Work in Modern Society*, London: SCM Press (for World Council of Churches) 1950.

Pieper, Josef, *Leisure: the Basis of Culture*, New York: Random House 1963.

Richardson, Alan, *The Biblical Doctrine of Work*, London: SCM Press 1952, 2nd ed. 1963.

Tilgher, A. , *Work. What It Has Meant through the Ages*, New York: Harcourt Brace, 1930.

Todd, John M. (ed.), *'Work', a Symposium*, London: Darton Longman & Todd 1960.

4 *Marriage, sex and the family*

Archbishop's Commission, *Marriage, Divorce and the Church*, London: SPCK 1971.

General Synod Marriage Commission, *Marriage and the Church's Task*, London: CIO 1978.

Harvey, A. E., *Promise or Pretence? A Christian's Guide to Sexual Morality*, London: SCM Press 1994.

Scruton, Roger, *Sexual Desire*, London: Weidenfeld & Nicolson 1986.

Sullivan, Andrew, *Virtually Normal: An Argument about Homosexuality*, London: Picador 1995.

Vasey, Michael, *Strangers and Friends: A New Exploration of Homosexuality and the Bible*, London: Hodder & Stoughton 1993.

5 *Human rights*

Bailey, Sydney D., *Human Rights and Responsibilities in Britain and Ireland*, London: Macmillan 1988.

Bailey, Sydney D., and Dawes, Sam, *The United Nations: A Concise Political Guide*, London: Macmillan 1995.

Finnis, J., *Natural Law and Natural Rights*, Oxford: Clarendon Press 1980.

Harvey, A. E., 'Human Rights: Rhetoric or Reality?', *Humanitas* 1, 1999, pp. 25–40.

Küng, Hans, and Moltmann, Jürgen, (eds), *The Ethics of World Religions and Human Rights*, *Concilium* 1991/2, London: SCM Press.

Küng, Hans, and Schmidt, Helmut, *A Global Ethic and Global Responsibilities*, London: SCM Press 1998.

Locke, John, *Two Treatises of Government*, ed. Peter Haslett, Cambridge: Cambridge University Press 1988.

Pontifical Commission, 'Justitia et Pax', *The Church and Human Rights*, Rome 1975.
Sieghart, Paul, *The Lawful Rights of Mankind*, Oxford: Oxford University Press 1985.

6 Volunteers and entrepreneurs

Himmelfarb, Gertrude, *The De-moralization of Society*, London: Institute for Economic Affairs 1995.
Jenkins. David E., *Market Whys and Human Wherefores*, London: Cassell 2000.
Leadbetter, Charles, *The Rise of the Social Entrepreneur*, London: Demos 1997.
Ormerod, Paul, *Butterfly Economics*, London: Faber & Faber 1998.

7 Indebtedness, stewardship and social justice

Mark, James, *The Question of Christian Stewardship*, London: SCM Press 1964.
Selby, Peter, *Grace and Mortgage*, London: Darton Longman & Todd 1997.
Taylor, Michael, *Not Angels but Agencies: The Ecumenical Response to Poverty – a Primer*, London: SCM Press; and Geneva: WCC 1995.
Yoder, John Howard, *The Politics of Jesus*, Grand Rapids: Eerdmans 1995.

8 Civil society

Green, David C., *Re-inventing Civil Society*, London: Institute for Economic Affairs 1993.
Keane, John, *Civil Society*, Oxford: Polity Press (Blackwell) 1998.
Putting Asunder: A Divorce Law for Contemporary Society, London: SPCK 1966.
Sacks, Jonathan, *The Politics of Hope*, London: Jonathan Cape 1997.
Seligman, Adam B., *The Idea of a Civil Society*, Princeton 1992.

9 Visions of the Kingdom

Berlin, Isaiah, *Four Essays on Liberty*, Oxford: Oxford University Press 1969.
Church of England Board for Social Responsibility, *Theology and Social Concern*, London 1986.
Gill, Robin, *Church-going and Christian Ethics*, Cambridge: Cambridge University Press 1999.
Harvey, A. E., *Retaliation: A Political and Strategic Option under Moral*

and Religious Scrutiny, Peterborough: Methodist Publishing House (for CCADD) 1992.

O'Donovan, Oliver, *The Desire of the Nations*, Cambridge: Cambridge University Press 1996.

Provost, James, and Wolf, Knut, *The Tabu of Democracy in the Church*, *Concilium* 5, 1992 London: SCM Press 1992.

Temple, William, *Christianity and Social Order*, London: Penguin 1942, 1956.

Wilkinson, Alan, *Christian Socialism: Scott Holland to Tony Blair*, London: SCM Press 1998.

10 Dangers of the bandwagon

Belo, F., *A Materialist Reading of the Gospel of Mark*, Maryknoll: Orbis 1977.

Harries, Richard, *Is There a Gospel for the Rich?* London: Mowbray 1992.

Murray, Robert, *The Cosmic Covenant: Biblical Themes of Justice, Peace and Integrity*, London: Sheed & Ward 1992.

Stendahl, Krister, 'Paul and the Introspective Conscience of the West', *Paul Among Jews and Gentiles*, London: SCM Press 1977.

Torrance, T. F., *Christian Theology and Scientific Culture*, New York: Oxford University Press 1981.

White, Lynn, *Machina ex Des*, ch. 5, Cambridge, Mass., London: MIT Press 1968.

11 Diversity and community

Church of England Board for Social Responsibility, *Church and Community Work*, 1988.

Edwards, David L., *Christians in a New Europe*, London: Collins 1990.

Etzioni, Amitai, *The Spirit of Community*, London: Fontana 1995.

Fergusson, David, *Community, Liberalism and Christian Ethics*, Cambridge: Cambridge University Press 1999.

Harvey, A. E., *Demanding Peace: Christian Responses to War and Violence*, London: SCM Press 1999.

Williamson, Roger (ed.), *Some Corner of a Foreign Field: Intervention and World Order*, London: Macmillan (for CCADD) 1998.

12 Epilogue: 'Go and do likewise'

Harvey, A. E., *Strenuous Commands: The Ethic of Jesus*, London: SCM Press 1990.

Hauerwas, Stanley, *After Christendom*, Nashville: Abingdon Press 1991.

Index of Names and Subjects

Trinity, the 27, 141
Turnbull Report 137–8

UN 105–6, 119
  Commissioner for Human
    Rights 64
  Convention (on children) 59
  Convention on Refugees 72
  Declaration of Human
    Rights 68–74, 109
unemployment 30, 36, 43–4
*Unemployment and the Future
  of Work* 36ff., 88
universality (of rights) 68–9
UPAs 4–5, 16ff.
urban theology 5, 23

usury 7
utilitarianism 117–8

Victim Support 81
virtue 46
voluntary sector 78ff.

war 144ff.
Water Buffalo Theology 13
wealth, creation of 136
welfare state 85–6
Wilkinson, Alan 129
Withymoor Surgery 86
work, 30ff.
  paid 44
Working as one Body 137–8
World Bank 91, 97

Index of Biblical References